WINES, BEERS and PARTY DRINKS

Consultants:

F. W. Beech
PhD DSc FRIC

Pat Cherry
NFWI Home Economics Adviser

Macdonald Educational in association with WI Books Ltd.

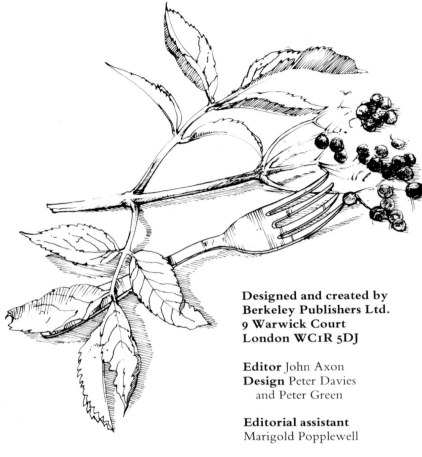

Equipment courtesy of:
Boots and Timothy Whites
Dartington Glass
4 Portland Road
London W11
W. R. Loftus Retail Limited
1 Charlotte Street
London W1
The Ravenhead Company
Limited
David Mellor
4 Sloane Square
London SW11

**Designed and created by
Berkeley Publishers Ltd.
9 Warwick Court
London WC1R 5DJ**

Editor John Axon
Design Peter Davies
and Peter Green

Editorial assistant
Marigold Popplewell

Photography Chris Ridley

Illustrations Gabrielle Stoddart

© WI Books Ltd. 1979

First published 1979
Macdonald Educational Ltd.
Holywell House
Worship Street
London EC2A 2EN

Editorial manager
Chester Fisher
Publishing co-ordinator
Gill Rowley
Production manager
Eva Wrennall

Made and printed by
Purnell & Sons Ltd., Paulton

ISBN 0 356 06310 0

The wine-maker and the law

English law states:
NO WINE MADE AT
HOME CAN BE SOLD
and
NO DISTILLATION CAN
TAKE PLACE.

The law in the UK is quite
clear. No wines made at
home may be sold, either
privately or to the public.
Nor may homemade wines
be offered for sale at bazaars,
jumble sales, home-produce
markets or church fêtes.

If you think that your
wine is good enough to be
sold, in the UK you must
obtain a licence from the
Customs and Excise Department and follow their
requirements in their
entirety. Failure to do so
could lead to heavy fines and
imprisonment.

HM Customs define wine
as any liquid made from
grapes, and 'homemade' as
that made from fruit and
sugar, mixed with any other
material which has gone
through a process of
fermentation.

Wine-makers outside the
UK should make themselves
familiar with their own
national laws covering wine-
making.

Contents

Preface

It is an interesting if macabre indication of the decline in real values over the centuries that the butt of Malmsey wine in which the Duke of Clarence is said to have been drowned in 1478 cost as little as a bottle of good burgundy would cost today. Wine-lovers will commiserate over this appalling waste of Malmsey and historians will no doubt forever speculate whether the story is true. But there can be no doubt at all about the increase in wine duty which has put up the price of what used to be one of life's more delightful indulgences into something approaching a pang of conscience. Wine today is expensive and wine-lovers must use their wits and their ingenuity if they are to carry on drinking.

The wine-lover really need not despair, for it is perfectly possible for an amateur with no previous experience of wine-making to make the most acceptable wines, given a little patience, practice and experience. Indeed, the whole range of wine varieties can be covered —apéritifs, table wines, dessert wines, what we might call 'social' wines for general drinking (apart from as an accompaniment to a meal), rosé wines and sparkling wines. And—the crowning joy and the spur to all inventive wine-makers—many of the main ingredients are free. All that is needed is some basic equipment: the financial outlay is small compared with the yield.

However, wine-making must be treated with respect. So, indeed, must everything in life that is really satisfying. Many wine-makers have developed their own special skills. Wine tastes can be very personal and skilled producers will have learned to suit their own individual palates. But if you follow the basic guidelines laid down in this book you will produce perfectly acceptable wine.

As many of the methods cited can be applied to more than one wine, this book makes use of a simple but effective system of cross-referencing. This should prove helpful to the beginner. The amateur can also make splendid beers, lagers and ciders, and all sorts of combinations of these for party drinks, following these recipes.

One word of warning to the beginner: do not be put off by the apparently scientific precision of the techniques described in this book. The implements you need are simple to use. You do not have to be a senior wrangler to work out quantities and you can be wholly ignorant of chemistry, physics and alchemy. All the necessary details are supplied to you. Mind you, once you have produced some bottles of a wine your friends pronounce to be delicious, you will feel rather like an alchemist who really did make gold. Making wine or good country ale or cider has this quality of satisfaction.

WI wine-makers have a long tradition of good winemaking. Their first book on homemade wines was published more than twenty years ago and WI members were making splendid wines a long time before that. And, of course, as good country people they were also making beers and ciders.

Homemade drinks represent not just a substantial saving on cost: they give you the satisfaction of using garden products and the fruits of the countryside to produce unique flavours and a well-stocked 'cellar' that will prove a continuing source of enjoyment.

F. W. Beech

A skill that started off with Noah

According to tradition, Noah planted the first vineyard. Since then, peasants, monks and monarchs have made their own wines. Home wine-making has a long and ancient history. Today wine-making is becoming increasingly popular. Within these pages you will find out how to make wines, what equipment you need and what ingredients to use for scores of traditional and new recipes. Here is a full guide to a skill which will spare your pocket and give you endless satisfaction.

The beginnings of wine-making

Early wines

Among the many remarkable things attributed to Noah, apart from building the Ark, was the planting of the world's first vineyard. True or false, it is an agreeable story for it seems entirely appropriate that a man who had the good sense to save all the world's animals should also have devised one of mankind's greatest blessings. Admittedly, he seems to have abused this in a bout of over-indulgence. Genesis goes on to tell us that 'he [Noah] drank of the wine and was drunken'. Otherwise, on the whole, the story of Noah and the first vineyard makes him a most sympathetic character.

We also know that the ancient Egyptians were just as dedicated to the vine, for tomb paintings show us that wine was commonly drunk in the Middle East at least 4,000 years ago. Nobody now knows what these wines were like, but there is some evidence that ancient wines were quite potent. The ancient Greeks regarded pure wine drinking as 'riotous', in that it led to riotous behaviour, and it was considered the gentlemanly thing to mix your wine with water. Only vulgar people took it neat. This tradition is still prevalent in certain parts of Europe.

Uncorked wine

In ancient times it was not possible to store wine for very long. A wine that was four years old was regarded as venerable. Greek wine was dark, which explains all those references to 'wine-dark seas' by Homer and other Greek poets. Bottles and corks had not been invented, and so the wine of the ancient world was kept in casks, goatskins or amphorae made of earthenware, and was stoppered by means of an oily or greasy rag. The result was that air was able to work effectively on the wine throughout its storage life. The Romans continued this method.

A hint of vintage

As the wealth of the Roman world grew, so did its wine connoisseurship. We are not sure what value standards applied, but it is clear from Roman literature that distinctions between vintages were made. We know that one vintage was particularly famous—that of 42 BC. But it is doubtful whether these ancient wines ever achieved the majestic quality of our best contemporary wines or of any of the great European vintages since the invention of the cork.

A fully matured wine was a virtual impossibility before the introduction of corks. We know that wine in a cask or any other vessel stoppered by an oily rag reaches maturity in about three years. Kept longer than that, in those storage conditions, it would not have improved, and would probably have deteriorated. Admittedly, hock is known to have been kept in casks for periods of up to twenty years until the end of the eighteenth century. According to contemporary opinion, its quality improved, but connoisseurs tend to be sceptical.

Monastic wines

Throughout the Dark Ages wine had steadily deteriorated in common with many other things, but the monks of that period were largely responsible for the reappearance of good wines with the development of monasteries. One cause of deterioration lay with the Romans. Wherever they went, the Romans took with them their habits and the things they most enjoyed. Baths were a blessing. So was the introduction of the apple tree to many parts of Europe and to Britain in particular. But the Romans were unfortunate with the wines they sought to establish in climates not really suited to the production of good vintages. Britain was one example, and in France the *vin de Suresne* was a by-word for thin wine.

Fortunately, the monks needed wine for the communion service and very properly concluded that poor, thin wine was something of an insult to the Creator. The medieval monarchs, princes and local potentates entirely shared this view and the cultivation of wine was increasingly left to the monks. It could

2

not have been left in better or more loving and capable hands.

Wine as medicine

Country wines were a most important part of the medieval rural medicine cupboard. Elizabethan women made far more wine than preserves, which they regarded as something of an indulgence. In any case, sugar was expensive in those days. Wine was considered as an indulgence which had 'medical' support. Elderberry wine was a specific against the coughs, colds and agues which must have plagued the draughty Elizabethan cottages. Cowslip wine was taken as a remedy for insomnia. It was, if you drank enough of it. Celery wine was said to work wonders for rheumatism and gout, both very common complaints in those days. A good glass of parsnip wine was recommended if the bowels were troublesome. Herbal wine helped to calm the nerves and was held to have a generally soothing effect.

The pop of corks

All wine-lovers should occasionally raise their glasses to toast the shade of Dom Pierre Perignon of Hautvillers, regarded as the father of the champagne trade, who developed the bottle and cork in the late seventeenth century. Dom Perignon's work made the dissemination of good bottled wine a possibility. Since those far-off days, wine has progressed considerably. Today there can be very few people who have not enjoyed wine at some time in their lives and most probably, wine of a far higher quality than any known to the heroes of Homer.

Here, we are not concerned with the great classic products of the vine. But it is pleasant for the modern country wine-maker to feel that he is working in a great tradition.

Homemade wine

Wine requires a great degree of respect from those who make it. Its production is not to be undertaken in any light or frivolous mood. Having taken a backward glance at monks and monarchs, and remembering in particular probably the greatest monarch of them all, Charlemagne, who is said to have

planted some of the most famous of the Rhenish and Burgundian vineyards, let us consider homemade country wines today. When so many splendid commercial wines are available, why should anyone bother to make homemade wine? One very obvious answer is cost. Today the price of good wine, thanks to the increasing depredations of the taxman, has rocketed.

But cost is not the only reason. Making wine is peculiarly satisfying as a hobby. Wine-makers are a breed apart. Inveterate devotees may be seen gazing intently at all sorts of blossoms, petals, fruits and vegetables with an abstract, musing air. Will it make a wine? Legends develop. Personality can actually be bottled and given to friends. For wine-making is a highly individualistic pastime and anyone with enough time and patience to spare can turn the common elderberry into a highly personalized drink, fit for a medieval monarch (and probably far too good for a Romanized Briton, reared on his thin and impoverished local wines). A wine-maker can now look at his roses with a new interest and grow lettuce to quench his thirst. He can view primroses with a more than poetic interest and become positively lyrical about bramble tips. Even pansies seem to wink encouragingly at him from their humble position in the garden borders, promising future pleasure.

The whole joy of homemade country wines lies in their infinite variety and rare possibilities. Provided the wine-maker follows a few simple and basic rules, the vegetable world is his oyster, which he can open up and turn into strange delights by means of a few simple implements and instructions.

Wine-making can, like the attempted transmutation of base metal by the alchemist of old, become addictive. But there is a difference. A modern home wine-maker can actually produce gold—not only liquid gold to be consumed, but also

money in his pockets from what he has saved in not buying wine.

The strange myth of the wine-giver god

Dionysus: who or what was he? Everyone knows that he was the god of wine in Greek mythology. But the wine god myth was widespread in pre-Christian societies and there is a close link between the cult of Dionysus and various Asiatic deities. Homer never refers to Dionysus as the originator of wine, but there is evidence that the name was familiar to the Greeks before 1200 BC.

Tradition has it that Dionysus was born at Thebes. He was supposed to be the son of Zeus by Semele (whose name means earth). Semele was foolish enough to ask Zeus to appear before her in his god-like form, but as Zeus was the god of lightning, the unfortunate Semele was killed by this manifestation. Zeus, however, rescued her baby, Dionysus, and enclosed him within his own thigh until he reached maturity. In this sense Dionysus can be said to have been born twice—a fate he shared with most classical gods connected with vegetation, in that he died and rose again, in some form.

Dionysus reputedly made an early world tour, teaching men how to grow the vine and encouraging them to practise his cult. However, the cult observances were not readily acceptable in polite society even in those uninhibited times. For instance, the king of Thebes took strong exception to some of the rites Dionysus urged upon the women of Thebes. Lycurgus, king of Thrace, also objected to the practices of the cult and Dionysus escaped his fury only by jumping into the sea. There are also stories of women who, having refused to join in the rites, were driven mad and

A fifteenth century illuminated manuscript showing Mr Noah in his vineyard and the gathering and pressing of grapes

transformed into bats.

There is a good deal of evidence of resistance to the Dionysean cult. Nevertheless, when Dionysus was kindly and hospitably treated, he responded by granting the gift of the vine to those welcoming him.

In various legends Dionysus' career can fairly be described as hectic. Often he appears in a tri-

A classic interpretation of the wine god Dionysus as a beautiful young man

umphal and conquering role. He figured as a conqueror of India by the time of Alexander the Great, and is also reputed to have turned an attacking pirate crew into a school of dolphins. He was also credited with prophetic powers and

5

Bacchus and revellers

at Delphi was apparently regarded as the equal of Apollo.

Dionysus is usually shown as a young man with an almost feminine form, except in the earliest representations, where he is bearded. The Dionysean or Bacchic myth occurs again and again in literature.

Keats refused to be '*charioted by Bacchus and his pards*', preferring what he called '*the viewless wings of poesy*'. Dryden took a more indulgent view and referred to '*Bacchus ever young and fair*'. The puritannical Milton made a truer assessment when he expressed his determination to '*drive far off the barb'rous dissonance of Bacchus and his revellers*'.

Predictably, that most sensuous of lyricists, Algernon Charles Swinburne, took a rather different line. '*Pan by noon and Bacchus by night, Fleeter of foot than the fleet-foot kid, Follows with dancing and fills with delight*'.

He goes on to describe '*the god pursuing the maiden hid*'.

But, as usual, the last word must

lie with Shakespeare, who makes no bones about his admiration for the god.

'Come, thou monarch of the vine,
Plumpy Bacchus, with pink eyne!
In thy fats, our cares be drown'd,
With thy grapes our hairs be crown'd:
Cup us, till the world go round,
Cup us till the world go round'.
Antony and Cleopatra

Country wine-makers are in excellent company so far as literature is concerned. Jane Austen—one of the most clear-thinking observers of the eighteenth-century social scene—makes a great many references to homemade wines. In her private letters to her sister Cassandra, she makes constant enquiries about the progress of various wines.

Jane denied being ruined by French wines when she wrote to Cassandra from her brother's home in Kent, and assured her that she would be home to help with the redcurrants. We know that the Austens made currant wine, orange wine, mead and even spruce beer. Other literary figures whose families made country wines include Thackeray, George Eliot and Mrs Gaskell, who mentions them in *Cranford*.

Equipment

The equipment you need can be considered in the following groups: measures, size reduction, extraction, fermentation, storage, bottling and dispensing, miscellaneous (see over).

Cleaning and sterilizing equipment

All the equipment should be kept scrupulously clean when not in use. If it becomes encrusted, bacteria and other organisms will grow which could spoil your next attempts. If ordinary domestic detergents and brushing fail to remove encrusted deposits, there are several excellent products on the market which will do this. Organic encrustation can be removed by oxidizing with a strong solution of domestic bleach. Containers can be sterilized with a mixture of Campden tablets and citric acid, followed by thorough washing and drying. If you are using proprietary detergents and sterilizing solutions, make sure that you follow the manufacturers' directions. The following solutions can also be used to clean your equipment.

Cleaning solutions

Proprietary detergents and sterilizing solutions should be used as directed by the manufacturer.

Soda solution
Dissolve 125 g (4 oz) washing soda in 5 litres (1 gall) boiling water

Hypochlorite solution
Mix 25 g (1 fluid oz) domestic bleach in 5 litres (1 gall) water

Sulphur dioxide solution
Dissolve six Campden tablets and 12 g ($\frac{1}{2}$ oz) citric acid in 575 ml (1 pint) water;

alternatively,
dissolve 7 g ($\frac{1}{4}$ oz) of sodium or potassium metabisulphite and 7 g ($\frac{1}{4}$ oz) of citric acid in 5 litres (1 gall) of water. Asthma-sufferers should avoid breathing in the sulphur dioxide given off by these solutions.

Equipment

Measures

Measuring cylinders (100 ml and 250 ml)
Graduated jug
Pipette
Kitchen scales
Balance and weights

Size reduction

Stainless steel knife
Chopping board
Hand grater
Kitchen grinder/mincer
Bowl
Potato masher
Liquidizer

Extraction

Colander
Jug
Juice extractor
Fruit press
Immersion heater
Thermostat
Buckets, bowls
Boiler with aluminium container
Trial tube hydrometer and jug

Fermentation
Plastic containers
Press cloth and fine sieve
Semi-rigid plastic containers
Glass jars and carboys
Plastic dustbins (containers)
Airlock and bung
Siphon tube/pump
Pinch clip

Bottling and dispensing
Corkers, hand and bench type
Bottles
Crown corks and corker
Funnels
Labels
Flanged, safety and champagne
corks
Screw tops
Beer cans
Bottle cleaning brushes

Storage
Filter bags and stand
Filter papers
Safety bungs

Drinking
Wine glasses
Carafe
Decanter

Acid and alkaline content of fruits and vegetables

Alkaline ash

Apples
Apricots, raw
Apricots, dried
Bananas
Blackberries, raw
Cherries, raw
Currants, raw
Dates, dried
Figs, dried
Gooseberries
Grapefruit
Grapes
Lemons
Loganberries
Nectarines
Oranges
Peaches, raw
Pears, raw
Pineapples, raw
Raisins
Raspberries, raw
Strawberries, raw
Tangerines, raw
Beetroot
Dandelion leaves
Lettuce
Parsnips
Potatoes

Acid ash

Cranberries
Plums
Prunes
Rhubarb

Type of acid content

Citric acid

bananas
blackcurrants
elderberries
grapefruit
lemons
oranges
pears
pineapples
raspberries
redcurrants
strawberries
white currants

Malic acid

apples
apricots
blackberries
cherries
damsons
gooseberries
greengages
loganberries
peaches
rhubarb (and oxalic acid)

Tartaric acid

grapes

Acidity of ingredients

Negligible

cereals
dates
figs
flowers
leaves
rosehips

Low

bananas
dried fruits
elderberries
pears
pineapples

Medium

apples
apricots
cherries
damsons
grapes
greengages
peaches

High

bilberries
blackberries
crab apples
gooseberries
loganberries
oranges
plums
quinces
raspberries
strawberries

Very high

blackcurrants
grapefruit
lemons
Morello cherries
redcurrants
rhubarb
white currants

Raw materials

The innocent might assume that all raw materials come from the field, garden or hedgerow. In fact, as the following list shows, more or less any raw material can be obtained, preserved by several of the classical methods. In addition, there are yeasts, adjuncts, finings, detergents and sterilizing agents.

Concentrated juices Grape— white, red or muscat, or specially formulated for particular wines; apple and orange. Unconcentrated canned juices, free from preservatives, made from lemon, orange and grapefruit, are also available.

Canned purees or pulps Apricot, peach, pineapple and rosehip.

Canned whole fruit Apricots, gooseberries, plums.

Dried flowers Dandelion, elderflower, parsley, red clover and rose petals.

Dried fruit Apricots, bananas, bilberries, cherries, dates, elderberries, figs, hawthorn berries, peaches, raisins, rosehips, sultanas.

Flavourings Caraway seed, ginger, juniper berries, vermouth powder (French and Italian).

Grains Barley, maize, rice and wheat. Flaked barley, maize, oats, rice and wheat. Crystal, lager, pale and roasted black malts. Malt and wheat flour.

Hops Fuggles, Golding, Northern Brewer, as well as imported varieties and concentrated hop extracts.

Sugars and syrups Glucose or dextrose (chips, powder and syrup), honey, malt (concentrate—either on its own or especially formulated with hop flavour—and spray-dried), sucrose (demerara, raw cane, sugar candy and white).

Fruits, herbs and vegetables

The raw materials for wine-making can mostly be found in your garden or in local fields and hedgerows. Fruits can be collected, and then preserved by either drying, bottling or canning until you are ready to use them. But if you intend to use fresh material, whether fruit, flowers,

leaves or vegetables, make sure it is really fresh and has not been contaminated in any way. This may seem obvious, but in these days of high pollution from motor vehicles, herbicides and pesticides, it is not easy to find material that is free from some form of pollution.

One golden rule is not to pick your material from hedgerows that flank roads, no matter how lush and productive they may seem. Choose plants growing well away from traffic routes: the internal combustion engine is a ubiquitous polluter and coughs out its lead fumes quite indiscriminately, with disastrous effects on all growing things. Choose quiet lanes undisturbed by traffic, or strike across country where the 'fields breathe sweet'.

Here again be cautious. Things are not always what they seem. Hedgerows flanking meadowland are reasonably safe, and so are isolated woodlands and copses. But hedgerows flanking growing crops may well have been sprayed with pesticides. Where you suspect pesticide spraying or any other form of contamination, avoid picking. Do not be seduced by ease of access or by the luscious berries.

Avoid fruit or other material which is rotting or mouldy or even 'on the turn'. Always use ingredients in the best condition, otherwise your wine will suffer from a mouldy flavour or will contain mycotoxins. The best time to pick fresh raw materials is when there has been very little rain for 24 hours. Wet fruit

A few raw materials to use in wine-making—but make sure your elderberries are ripe and black

and vegetables can become mouldy very quickly, giving unpleasant wine.

It is essential that the raw materials you use should have a pleasant flavour and sufficient sugar, either natural or added. If sugar is lacking, the required amount of alcohol will not be produced during the fermentation process.

The quantity of sugar required will depend on the final alcoholic content required in the wine you are making. A useful guide is that a dry white table wine should contain about 10 per cent of alcohol by volume and a dessert wine between 12 and 15 per cent (see Model Wine page 18). The fruit's natural sugar content is usually ignored unless you are using a very sweet fruit.

In the recipes detailed ingredients lists are given, but generally for dry wines 1 kg (2¼ lb) white sugar is added for every 4·5 litres (1 gall) water, and 1·2 kg (2¾ lb) sugar for sweet wines. If brown sugar or honey is used, increase the amount of sugar by 50 per cent.

Water is not usually a problem, though there are some points to watch. Tap water is usually quite suitable unless you happen to live in an area which draws its water from a peaty source. In that case the flavour may not be affected, but the colour will be. Also avoid heavily chlorinated water supplies.

Adjuncts
Acids Citric, malic and tartaric.
Enzymes Amylase (for starch), Rohament P (for breaking up tissue) and Pectolase, Pectozyme, Pectinol, Klerzyme, Ultrazyme 100 (for pectin).
Sulphite Campden tablets, sodium and potassium metabisulphite.
Yeast food Ammonium phosphate or sulphate, thiamin, vitamin B complex and proprietary mixtures.

13

Fining agents
Bentonite
Gelatine (leaf or powder) normally used in conjunction with tannin.
Irish moss or carragheen—used for clarifying beer.

Cleaning agents
Detergents Domestic Silana PF.
Sterilizing agent Domestic hypochlorite.

Water treatment
Usually a mixture of inorganic salts used in brewing that reduces the pH rapidly during fermentation in order to inhibit bacteria.

Yeasts
These can be obtained for a variety of purposes: beer (ale or lager), general purpose wine yeast, champagne, port, madeira, mead, sauternes, sherry. Available as liquid cultures or slurries, as growth on agar media, or dried in the form of granules, powders or tablets.

Ingredients
Potential ingredients are legion, but in case rural walks are not your line, plenty of basic materials are available in the shops. You do not have to become a cross-country hearty! You can also easily obtain all the yeasts, adjuncts, finings, detergents and sterilizing agents you will need. A wealth of specialized equipment is readily available today at modest prices in some chemists and other shops all over the country. The introduction of special kits has taken most of the hard labour out of wine-making. Newcomers might be well advised to start their wine-making careers by using one of these kits. The instructions are easy to follow and a wide variety of wine types is available—hocks, clarets, burgundies. You can also buy cans of blended grape concentrate, which needs only the addition of water, sugar and the yeast culture provided to produce drinkable wine.

From this simple starting point, you can proceed to make wine from fresh fruits and vegetables and some of the more exotic substances we feature in this book. We hope you will, for wine has a pervasive and infectious personality. Once you have mastered the first principles, we hope you will proceed with ever-increasing cunning and confidence, and in due course enjoy the fruit of your labours and the adulation of your guests.

Types of wine
At the start you should consider what type of wine you wish to make. Is it to be dry or sweet, dark or light? Do you wish your wine to be a mealtime accompaniment, or is it to be used on social occasions? These points are important. To help you, we begin this book with a classification chart. All wines must follow certain basic rules in the making.

Many of the instructions that follow are common to all the wines we list. To help you, we have divided our recipes into groups. There are basic rules common to each group. To make the wine of your choice, look it up in the classification table, turn to the recipe for the ingredients and then follow the basic rules for that group.

Perfection and the personal touch given by inspired experimentation come with experience. For your first attempts, stick to simple recipes using freely available materials. And observe a few simple rules. Never use equipment with copper, iron, cadmium, lead or zinc surfaces. These could not only damage your health but could also affect the colour and flavour of your wine. Some plastics are unsuitable for wine-making. Use only those sold specifically for wine-making purposes.

Poisonous Plants

A   acacia, aconite, alder, anemone, aquilegia, azalea
B   baneberry, belladonna, berberis, bitter almond, bay tree leaves, beech nuts, box tree leaves, black nightshade, bindweed, bluebell, bryony, broom, buckthorn, buddleia, buttercup
C   campion, celandine, charlock, cineraria, clematis, clover, cotoneaster, columbine, cowbane, crocus, crowfoot, chrysanthemum, cuckoopint, cyclamen
D   daffodil, dahlia, deadly nightshade, delphinium, dwarf elder
F   fool's parsley, figwort, foxglove, fungi
G   geranium, gladioli, goosefoot, green potatoes
H   helebore, hemlock, henbane, holly, honeysuckle, horse chestnut, hydrangea, hyacinth
I   iris, ivy
J   jasmine, jonquil
L   laburnum, laurel, lilac, lillies, lilies of the valley, lobelia, lucerne, lupins
M   marsh marigolds, meadow rue, mezereon, mistletoe, monkshood
N   narcissus
O   orchids
P   pheasant's eye, peony, poppy, privet
R   ragwort, rhododendron, rhubarb leaves
S   snowdrop, spearwort, spindleberries, spurge, sweet pea
T   thorn apple, tobacco plant, tomato stems and leaves, traveller's joy, tulip
W   wood anemone, woody nightshade
Y   yew

Herbs

Herbal wines were highly prized in the Middle Ages for their medicinal virtues, although a good many of them were rather slow in their curative effects. Before the days of antibiotics, people were used to slow cures and herbal wines were exceptionally pleasant medicines.

There is a discreet reference by Nicholas Culpeper in the book *A Physicall Directory* (1649) to a herb concoction known as 'bitter wine', which was said to help 'in the evil that Venus and her wanton girls produce'. It was also supposed to cure jaundice. But bitter wine is not to everyone's taste, no matter how curative its content.

Balsam, known to the Romans and other ancient civilizations as balm, has always been acclaimed for its soothing effects. It also has a delicate and delightful fragrance.

Parsley wine is said to be good for rheumatism, and celery also is supposed to benefit this affliction. Both make a light wine that is not only refreshing but has a most delicate flavour.

Parsnip

The parsnip is a native of Europe and has been cultivated since Roman times. A wild form, with a tough and very pungent root, is found along roadsides throughout Europe. The parsnip only reached America in the seventeenth century.

The parsnip is a remarkably hardy plant: even a hard freezing of the soil does not damage its root. Cold conditions produce a remarkable change in the parsnip. At the end of the summer, the solids in the root consist mainly of starch but after several weeks' exposure to near-freezing temperatures, much of this starch content is turned into sugar, which considerably improves the plant's culinary qualities.

Bilberry

Bilberry is the main food of grouse, as the shrub flourishes on heathland and in open woods and copses.

It is chiefly found in the hilly areas of Britain and northern Europe and Asia. The American blueberry of blueberry pie fame is of the same family but, unlike the cultivated blueberry, the wild bilberry bears its berries singly. The bilberry has small, globular flowers of a rosy colour, tinged with green. The berries, which are a dark blue, ripen in late summer.

In addition to wine, bilberry makes splendid tarts and is also popular as a preserve.

Gooseberry

The gooseberry is a close relative of the currant and was cultivated in English gardens as early as the seventeenth century. Many different varieties are now grown throughout the northern hemisphere, although as a food the gooseberry is far more important in Northern Europe than in North America. Europeans eat gooseberries in their natural state as well as using them in preserves. The North Americans use the fruit mostly in jellies, preserves and pies.

The gooseberry has also given its name to grossularite, the so-called 'gooseberry garnet' whose greenish colour and rounded shape bears a close resemblance to the fruit.

Strawberry

The strawberry, in a botanical sense, is not a berry at all. It is a greatly enlarged stem end containing the plant's seeds.

Water accounts for 90 per cent of the weight of strawberries. A cupful of strawberries yields about 90 calories.

Strawberries are rich in Vitamin C. They contain more of this vitamin than an equal quantity of lemons. A handful of freshly picked strawberries contains sufficient Vitamin C to sustain a healthy adult for a day. They also contain more Vitamin A than the equivalent weight of raisins. The large-fruited cultivated strawberry originated in Europe in the eighteenth century but the wild woodland strawberry had long been popular in England, France and Italy.

Strawberries easily perish and must be stored in cool, dry places, but they should not be refrigerated. The USA produces as many strawberries as the whole of Western Europe.

Juice extraction

Having collected your ingredients
and decided that the water supplies
come up to standard, the next step is
to extract the juice. Methods vary
because you cannot, for example,
squeeze a potato in the same way
that you can squeeze a strawberry.
There are also flowerheads to be
considered. Flowerheads and leaves
should be steeped for a time in the
fermenting sugar water. Vegetables, on the other hand, are normally diced and boiled until they
are soft. While they are boiling,
soluble pectin is extracted from the
vegetables. This has to be broken

down by the addition of special enzymes sold for the purpose.

In the recipes that follow, we give
the quantities of enzymes necessary
if you are using Pectozyme. Ultrazyme 100, Pectinol, Pektolase, Klerzyme and others are also easily
available. If you are using these, follow the amounts recommended by
the manufacturers.

For those interested in the tech-
nical aspects, the enzymes destroy
the pectin by breaking it down into
small, soluble molecules of galac-
turonic acid. If the pectin were not
broken down, the final wine would
be hazy and unattractive. Enzymes

may not, theoretically, be necessary
if your raw material is a cold water
extract of fruit. This is because the
natural enzymes of the fruit and the
yeast combine to destroy the pectin.
But proprietary enzymes are recommended as their action is much
quicker. With some soft fruits, the
enzyme must be added to the
crushed fruit before any juice can be
liberated, in which case instructions
are given in the recipes.

Juice can be extracted from fruit
by cooking it in a double saucepan,
or by using a commercial fruit-
master. These methods of juice extraction break the cells down by

Juice treatment

Having extracted the juice, the next task is to treat it. Unfortunately, the raw ingredients contain not only juice and colouring agents but also moulds, yeasts, bacteria and the nutrients on which these feed. Oxydizing enzymes are also present which, if not inhibited, would produce an unpleasant dark wine. These undesirables could be destroyed by boiling the pulp or the extract, but this process would dissolve the pectin and perhaps cause protein hazes in the final wines. Boiling could also affect the delicacy and subtlety of flavour.

For this reason, the unwanted organisms are destroyed by treating the extract with sulphur dioxide. Different degrees of acidity in the extract require different amounts of sulphur dioxide (see Acidity charts). It is necessary to add the amount of sulphur dioxide and acid that will produce the required amount of active (or free) sulphur dioxide (SO_2) for each type of wine. Here, the wonders of modern science come to the aid of the wine-maker in the form of Campden tablets, which contain Osalde sulphur dioxide.

Our recipes tell you if (and how many) Campden tablets are required for the wine being made. Always allow 12 hours after the tablets have been added before adding the yeast. This is because the SO_2 would react with the yeast as well as destroying the unwanted enzymes, moulds and bacteria, and so delay the start of fermentation.

heat and liberate the juice. Stone fruits are normally broken down by pouring boiling water over the fruit and squeezing the resulting pulp through muslin, a nylon cloth, or a small screw press. Coloured juices are not necessarily obtained from red fruits by direct pressing. It is necessary to ferment some fruits, such as black grapes or blackcurrants, on the skins. This is because the colour is concentrated in the skins, not in the natural juices of the fruit.

Treading the grapes—a mediaeval woodcut

Sugar content

Specific Gravity	Metric g in 4·5 litres	Imperial oz in 1 gall	% Alcohol	Baume	Twadell
1·125	1,334	47	16·98	16·0	25
1·120	1,275	45	16·30	15·5	24
1·115	1,232	43½	15·62	14·9	23
1·110	1,190	42	14·95	14·3	22
1·105	1,134	40	14·27	13·7	21
1·100	1,078	38	13·57	13·1	20
1·095	1,035	36½	12·90	12·5	19
1·090	994	35	12·23	11·9	18
1·085	937	33	11·55	11·3	17
1·080	880	31	10·87	10·7	16
1·075	822	29	10·19	10·0	15
1·070	780	27½	9·50	9·4	14
1·065	723	25½	8·83	8·8	13
1·060	680	24	8·15	8·2	12
1·055	624	22	7·47	7·5	11
1·050	567	20	6·79	6·9	10
1·045	510	18	6·10	6·2	9
1·040	453	16	5·43	5·5	8
1·035	396	14	4·75	4·9	7
1·030	339	12	4·07	4·2	6
1·025	283	10	3·40	3·5	5
1·020	226	8	2·70	2·8	4
1·015	170	6	2·04	2·1	3
1·010	113	4	1·39	1·4	2
1·005	50	2	0·69	0·7	1

Model wines

Category	Type	% Alcohol	Model
White table wine	light	9·5–10·5	Moselle
	light–medium	10·0–11·5	Hock
	medium	10·0–11·5	Reisling
	dry	11·0–13·0	Chablis
	medium–sweet	12·0–14·0	Graves
	full-bodied sweet	12·0–14·0	Sauternes
White dessert wine	full-bodied	12·0–14·0	Muscat
	sweet (full-bodied)	12·0–14·0	Barsac
	full-bodied sweet	12·0–15·0	Sauternes
Red table/social	light fruity medium	10·5–12·5	Beaujolais
Red table wine	medium-bodied, dry	11·5–12·0	vin ordinaire
	medium-full bodied, dry	12·0–14·0	Bordeaux
	full-bodied, dry	12·0–14·0	Burgundy
	full-bodied, dry, fruity	13·0–16·0	Rhône

CENTIGRADE | FAHRENHEIT

Yeast table

Ingredient	Wine type	Yeast recommended
Apple	sparkling	Champagne
	sweet	Sauternes
Apricot	dry	Chablis
	sweet	Sauternes
Blackberry	dry	Burgundy
	sweet	Port
Blackcurrant	dry	Burgundy
	sweet	Port
Damson	dry	all-purpose
	sweet	Port
Elderberry	dry	Burgundy
	sweet	Port
Gooseberry	dry	Chablis
	sweet	all-purpose
Loganberry	dry	Burgundy
	sweet	Port
Orange	dry	Chablis
	sweet	Sauternes
Peach	dry	all-purpose
	sweet	Sauternes
Pear	sweet	all-purpose
Plum	sweet	Madeira
Raspberry	sweet	all-purpose
Redcurrant	dry	Bordeaux
Rhubarb	sweet	all-purpose
Flowers	sweet	all-purpose
Tree sap	sweet	all-purpose
Vegetables	sweet	all-purpose

Adjustment to SG

	50	122
	45	113
	40	104
	35	95
+6.8	30	86
+5.0	25	77
+3.4	20	68
+2.0	15	59
+1.0	10	50
nil	5	41
−0.6	0	32

.... Ferment wines
Serve red table wines/dessert wines

.... Serve white/rose table wines/sparkling wines

Temperature/Specific Gravity adjustments
Different temperatures cause variations in reading SG

Yeast culture

Most wine-makers use commercial preparations of wine yeast which are sold as powders, tablets, granules, liquid suspensions or as growths on nutrient agar slopes. All of these are easily available. Whichever you decide to use, you must rack, or siphon, the wine from the yeast deposit as soon as possible after fermentation has finished.

Different types of yeast are available (see Yeast page 19) but do not expect a Sauternes yeast automatically to produce a Sauternes wine, nor a Chablis yeast a Chablis wine. It all depends on the ingredients and methods you use.

Different yeasts have different characteristics which the wine-maker will come to know as he becomes proficient. The yeast charts provide further information, however.

The retailer is usually happy to give advice on which particular yeasts are suitable for high alcohol content, SO_2 tolerance and quick fermentation. If you are a beginner, you will be well advised to use a general-purpose yeast culture and

Nutrients
Just as a soil needs fertilizer, so yeast needs its nutrients. Some wine-makers do not mind acid and nitrogenous matters in the fruit pulp. Others use a prepared commercial nutrient, according to the amount recommended by the manufacturer. Or you can add 5 ml (1 teaspoon) ammonium sulphate per 5 litres (1 gall).
The simplest nutrient mix for 5 litres (1 gall) dry wine is 1 mg thiamin hydrochloride and 2 g ammonium sulphate, and for sweet wines 1 mg thiamin hydrochloride and 4 g ammonium sulphate, which produces a highly alcoholic dessert wine.

then see how it behaves for different types of wines. This type of culture should ferment any wine to dryness in a reasonable time. It should settle out as a firm deposit at the end of fermentation and should not form any unpleasant odours.

Do not be afraid of experimenting with your yeasts. A sweetened extract can be divided into two, and the two halves can be fermented with different yeast cultures. In this way, you will build up a good working knowledge of yeasts.

The amount of yeast you should use will be given on the packet. Your original yeast can be used several times over and increased in quantity. To do this, boil up a small amount of the original mix. Pour this, while still hot, into a baby's toughened-glass feeding bottle.

of mix, again 12 hours after sulphit-ing. The main criterion is that the yeast culture should be increased in volume as soon as it is in an active state of fermentation. However, do not use the original culture too many times. Always return to a pure yeast starter at regular intervals.

General-purpose yeast cultures

To begin with, use a general-purpose yeast culture and see how it behaves for different wines. It should ferment the wine to dryness in a reasonable time. It should also settle out as a firm deposit at the end of fermentation and not form any unpleasant off-odours. For interest, a sweetened extract can be divided into two and the two halves fermented with different yeast cultures. In this way a working knowledge of the yeasts can be obtained under real conditions.

If you are in any doubt as to the amount of yeast to be used, the initial starter can be increased in quantity by boiling up a small amount of the original mix and pouring while hot into a baby's toughened-glass feeding bottle. Stopper this with non-absorbent cotton wool and, when the mix is cool, inoculate with dried yeast granules. After a little while at 21°C (70°F), the yeast will be activated and can then be poured into 5 litres (1 gall) mix, 12-24 hours after sulphiting.

The main criterion is that the yeast culture should be increased in volume as soon as it is in an active state of fermentation.

Yeast eats itself to increase

When it is cool, plug the bottle with non-absorbent cotton wool and add some yeast. Keep the bottle at a temperature of 21°C (70°F) which is sufficient to activate the yeast after a short time. Pour this into 5 litres (1 gall) of mix 12 hours after the Campden tablets have been added. Once this begins to work, it can be mixed with up to 40·5 litres (9 gall)

Yeast

What is yeast? It took one of the most celebrated scientific battles of the nineteenth century to establish that yeast was a living substance.

For years its function in alcoholic fermentation was a matter of great argument. It was left to the great French chemist and microbiologist Louis Pasteur (1822-95) to establish and define the precise activity of this tiny, microscopic, single-celled plant organism which thrives all over the world in soil and on plant surfaces. His work led to the germ theory of disease with all the vast consequences of that break-through. He established that fermentation is a chemical change which occurs within the cells of micro-organisms. It took forty years of detailed research to determine the complex nature of chemical fermen-tation.

The ancient world knew about the action of fermen-tation and of the ability of many yeasts to convert sugar into alcohol, but they had no idea of the nature of the process. Yeast was not even regarded as a specific substance until the nineteenth century. Nobody knew that it was, in fact, an organism with extraordinary powers of chemical catabolism.

Yeast is a very valuable food substance, rich in protein and in vitamins of the B group. When fresh yeast is allowed to age it has the extraordinary ability to digest itself and so lose its viability.

Fermentation conditions

As a general rule, the higher the temperature, the faster the rate of fermentation. Most yeasts will die if the temperature is allowed to rise to more than 30°C (85°F), although Tokay yeast has been used for fermentation at 37°C (100°F). The safe maximum temperature is generally held to be 25°C (77°F). Sometimes other considerations dictate the fermentation temperature. Red wines produce maximum colour at a fermented temperature of 27-28°C (80-82°F). Similarly, white wines are fermented at 21°C (70°F).

Campden tablets destroy the unwanted micro-organisms contained in the raw materials. After six hours, 90 per cent of the unwanted organisms are removed, and most of the remainder are killed off during the next 18 hours. Therefore, you should never yeast until at least 12 hours after adding Campden tablets.

When the yeast is added, it lies dormant at first. The cultures may slightly decrease in number until they get used to their new surroundings. When this happens, the individual cells begin to take up the dissolved oxygen, soluble nitrogenous compounds, sugars, vitamins and mineral salts. Each cell then produces a bud which grows until it is the same size as the 'mother' cell. The mother then produces a new bud and so does the daughter. Eventually, the number of yeast cells increases sufficiently to give a fermenting population when all the dissolved oxygen is exhausted.

At this point fermentation begins, when sugar yields equal weights of ethyl alcohol and carbon dioxide gas. It is at this stage that by-products are formed: fusel oils (or alcohols larger than ethyl alcohol) and organic acids. The exact amounts are determined by the types of yeasts which are used, the temperature, and conditions of fermentation. Sometimes these by-products can adversely affect the acidity of the wine, or the speed of fermentation, which is why we add nutrients such as ammonium salts and thiamin to the wine, especially to low nutrient juices. The amounts of commercial nutrient mixtures required are given on the packet labels. Otherwise, a general rule is to add 2-4 g BP-quality ammonium sulphate and 1 mg thiamin per 4·5 litres (1 gall).

Fermentation produces bubbles of carbon dioxide which rise in the liquid and with some of the yeast cells form the yeast head. First fermentation is normally carried out in an open-mouthed fermenting vessel covered with a sheet of polythene film. When froth formation has ceased, the liquid is racked into fermenting jars and allowed to continue to ferment under an airlock.

When the gas bubbles cease to form, the wine should be tasted. If it is dry or has reached the required degree of sweetness, remove the jars to a cool place for the specified

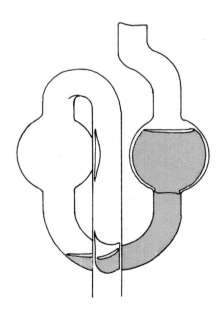

An airlock showing how the water within is pushed to the outside during fermentation.

length of time. If you are not happy with the colour, flavour or degree of dryness, there are several steps that you can take (see Faulty fermentation page 30).

Subsequent treatment of the wine will depend on the type you wish to produce. Dry wine should be kept as cool as possible to allow the yeasts to separate out. It is then siphoned off the yeast deposit into a storage jar. This storage jar should be corked or stoppered with a safety storage bung, and kept cool for at least three months or until the wine clarifies completely (for wines that fail to clarify, see Hazes page 30).

Sweet wines have to be stabilized so that they do not re-ferment in their final bottle. To achieve this stabilization, add sugar to the fully fermented wine at the rate of 225 g per 5 litres (8 oz per 1 gall). Replace the air lock and return the wine to a warm place. Repeat this until the concentration of sugar and alcohol prevents the yeast from working. Once this point has been reached, you proceed as for dry wines.

When the wine is completely clarified, it should be run off into bottles and corked. White and rosé wines can be further treated at this stage by adding one Campden tablet to every 5 litres (1 gall). The bottles should be left standing upright overnight and should then be stored on their sides for the necessary length of time. Check for any signs of leakage. Ensure that the storage temperature does not exceed 15°C (60°F). Wines that are sealed with plastic corks are best stored upright.

The wine can alternatively be dispensed into a plastic cask fitted with a run-off tap. If you decide to do this, fit a CO_2 injection unit to the top of the cask. This ensures an atmosphere of carbon dioxide over the top of the wine and prevents any unwanted oxidative changes.

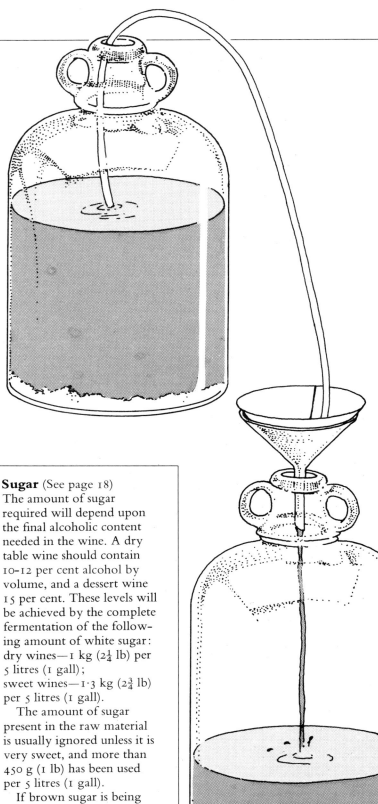

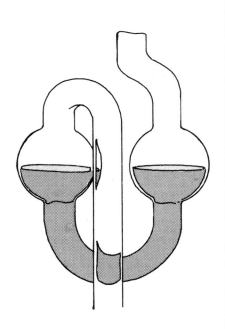

When fermentation has stopped, the water in the airlock will balance out on either side.

Sugar (See page 18)
The amount of sugar required will depend upon the final alcoholic content needed in the wine. A dry table wine should contain 10-12 per cent alcohol by volume, and a dessert wine 15 per cent. These levels will be achieved by the complete fermentation of the following amount of white sugar:
dry wines—1 kg ($2\frac{1}{4}$ lb) per 5 litres (1 gall);
sweet wines—1·3 kg ($2\frac{3}{4}$ lb) per 5 litres (1 gall).

The amount of sugar present in the raw material is usually ignored unless it is very sweet, and more than 450 g (1 lb) has been used per 5 litres (1 gall).

If brown sugar is being used the amounts used will be approximately 50 per cent greater than those given.

Wine descriptions

(not guaranteed to fall within the terms of the Trade Descriptions Act)

acerbe	sharp, acid, thin
acid	unsweet, not sour; fresh (of young wines)
aroma	fragrance of wine on exposure to air
balance	poised, equal qualities of a wine
body	degree of substance/wateriness
bouchonné	corky, unfit to drink
bouquet	the mixture of smells (of any wine); the grape and fermentation smell (original bouquet); the developed smell (applied bouquet)
bouqueté	having a lot of bouquet
breed	distinguished of its sort
complet	rounded out, lacking nothing
corsé	having a lot of tannin, full-bodied, of character
délicat	light, fine, not weak
doux	sweet; unfortified, natural sweet wines over 14 per cent alcohol (vins doux naturel, VDN)
élégant	well-balanced, distinctive, not heavy

étoffé	full
fat	having a lot of bouquet and little body
finesse	of delicate taste; of excellent development; finely balanced
floweriness	light, like flower smells; of the original bouquet, smell and taste of the grapes
franc de goût	simple in taste, clean, direct
fruitiness	strong smell or taste of the grape; full
fraîche	fresh-tasting; with agreeable acidity
full	large in bouquet or taste; not light of watery
généreux	full, rich, big
goût de cave	heavy, unpleasant taste
goût de terrain	pleasant taste of the vineyard soil
légèreté	lightness
mâché	big, full, filling the mouth
madérizé	a rusted, or oxidized white wine; undrinkable
moelleux	full of body and flavour, mellow
mordant	pleasant, biting sensation, due to acidity
nerveux	big, full wine
oeil de perdix	colour of a rosé wine; pale as the eye of a partridge
parfumé	perfumed, fresh, full
racé	distinctive, true to type
robé	large, full bouquet
sec	dry, not sweet; positive characteristic of light wines
seché	too dry; too acid
sève	pleasant smoothness from glycerine developed by yeast fermentation
souplesse	suppleness, soft, smooth
soyeux	silky; neither harsh nor bitter
suave	smooth, full
tendre	soft; neither harsh nor sharp
velouté	velvety, full, rich

Wine labels

Trade abbreviations—for authentic-type labels

A	Amontillado
alc	alcohol
A⁰	A^0 anno (year)
Artis	artisans
Bbn	Bourbon
BEB	best ever bottled
Bord/x	Bordeaux
BPS	British plain spirits
bot	bottle/bottled
Burg	Burgundy
CE	*Cuvée extra*
Ch	Château
Champ	Champagne
D	distillery
Dom	domestic
DOM	*Deo optimo maximo* (to god, most good, most great)
E–B	estate-bottled
Et	*établissement*
Ex	extra
FC	fine Champagne
FO	fine old
FOB	fine old blend
FOES	fine old extra special
MdCh	*mis du château*
NPU	*ne plus ultra*
NV	non-vintage
op	over proof
orig	original
pf	proof
pg	proof gallon
Saut	Sauternes
SFC	superior fine cognac
SO	superior old
sup	*Supérieur*
up	under proof
VdeP	*Vino de pasto*
VFC	very fine cognac
vint	vintage
VO	very old
VOP	very old pale
VOT	very old tawny
VOX	very old Jerez
VS	very superior
VSO	very superior old/ very special old
VSOP	very superior old pale
Vve	*Veuve* (widow)
VVO	very very old
VVS	very very superior

Wine etiquette

The few old-fashioned rules of wine service (etiquette) are simple.

At home The host (never the hostess) opens the wine and usually pours a small amount into his own glass, so that he will get any broken cork, if unfortunately there is some (and it has been known with both château- and home-bottled vintages). If there is a waiter, or butler, at hand, he will pour the first of the wine into the glass of the host, who is then expected to smell it politely, and maybe taste it (not necessary unless he has lost his sense of smell). The host will then nod his approval to the waiter. Provided he does not detect any of the faults listed in our table of faults— such as wrong colour, a haze condition, a smell of rotten eggs, or any of the other things that we have indicated may happen to your wine (and why and how to avoid them), the waiter will then serve the female guests, the male guests and lastly the host. After the first bottle, the host may pour. Or he may ask one of the men to do it for him, if more convenient, and if the occasion is not a formal one.

In a restaurant After taking the wine order, the wine-waiter should bring the bottle to the host for him to check that at least the label is correct (château, vintage, colour, proof), the bottle shape authentic, and the etiquette (seal over the cork) intact. If the host approves, the waiter then uncorks the bottle and pours the first of the wine into the glass of the host, who then smells it discreetly but knowingly, and approves, or tastes it and nods. The guests are served, ladies first, but without advantage as it is usual for the host to take the first sip to signify that the wine is ready for drinking. Wine is usually served after the soup course.

At a buffet The host usually pours the first glass of wine. The bottles are generally left on the sideboard for guests to help themselves (self-service) or be served by the waiters (waiter-service).

Intimate dinner It is customary for the man to pour the wine for his female partner, whether he is the host or guest. By tradition (that is before the liberation movement), a woman would never pour her own wine in a man's presence, even if she were served a separate carafe.

Hostless occasions The hostess will ask a male guest to pour the wine (unless liberated, or without a male guest).

Formal occasion The appropriate wine is poured after each course has been served. The glass should not be more than half filled. A separate, and often different, type of glass should be set and used for each wine served.

The categories of wine

We have divided the wines in this book into six categories.

Aperitif

This is a wine that can be drunk by itself before a meal and which stimulates the appetite.

Table wine

This is a wine suitable for accompanying a meal. In general it should not be too strong in bouquet and flavour and its alcoholic content should be about 10-12 per cent by volume. Usually, table wine is lighter in body and drier than social and dessert wines.

Dessert wine

This wine can be white, golden, red or tawny. It needs to be rich in bouquet and flavour, medium-to-sweet, full-bodied and of a high alcoholic content. By custom, this wine is served at the end of a meal.

Social wine

This is a wine that is intended for drinking other than with a meal. It usually possesses more flavour, and is sweeter than a table wine.

Rose wine

A rosé should be pink, delicate in bouquet and flavour, light in texture and alcoholic content and it should be medium dry. Rosé wine is suitable for serving chilled at table with many dishes.

Sparkling wine

This wine contains carbon dioxide, produced by a secondary fermentation in the bottle.

The colour of wines
Red wines

Red wines offer a variety of colour and flavour, ranging from the brilliant red of redcurrant wine to the purple red of the elderberry wines. This is one of the reasons why they are so popular with wine-makers. The actual depth of the colour can be varied in two ways: first, by the amounts of fruit used for each unit volume, and secondly by the method of pulp treatment.

Very few red fruits have red juice. The colouring is in the skins and in order to produce red wines, this colouring must be extracted. Normally the fruit is pulped and allowed to ferment with the skins, as alcohol, formed during yeast fermentation, is one of the best of solvents. Before pulping, strigs are removed, as they can impart a bitterness to the final

the beginner to make. However, do not worry if your initial attempts at producing rosé wines end in disaster. It is a common fate for beginners.

The easiest way to make a rosé wine is to blend a light red wine with an unoxidized white wine. But this is to adopt too simple a solution. Some fruits, such as certain varieties of plums and strawberries, produce a naturally pale red wine, but the colour is not the pure pink of commercial rosé wines. The true pink colour can be achieved by mixing the pulp of red-fleshed fruit with a suitable amount of white-fleshed fruit. It is also possible to produce rosé wine by fermenting the pulp of black- or red-skinned fruits for a maximum of three days. Or the pulp of these fruits can be soaked in unoxidized white wine until the desired colour is produced. We give several recipes for rosé table and dessert wines. Try them. All are well worth drinking.

The classification for the type of wine is given with the recipes.

White wines

There are two major classes of homemade white wines—water-white wines made from apples, white gooseberries, white grapes or white currants, and pale fawn to fawn wines which use herbs, flowers, vegetables, apricots, raisins and figs.

White wines should not normally be kept for more than a couple of years. Under these two main categories come the unoxidized light table wines, light fawn table wines, full-bodied fawn table wines and dessert fawn wines. We give a variety of recipes for each type.

As with red and rosé wines, the classification of the type of wine is given with the recipes.

Sparkling wines

Sparkling wine always produces a sense of 'occasion'. To make an acceptable sparkling wine, choose a wine that is fresh in flavour, dry and newly racked after its first fermen-

wine. This is especially true of the strigs of elderberries which, if left to ferment, would affect the final flavour to such an extent that even the most ardent wine-lover would find the wine undrinkable.

The rate of colour extraction can be accelerated by pouring boiling water over the fruits or by adding pectin-destroying enzymes six hours before yeasting. The alcohol and carbon dioxide, formed during fermentation, extract the colouring from the pulped skins. Initially, the pulp turns a greyish purple, but the full, rich colour is soon restored, once fermentation begins.

The fermenting pulp should be stirred several times a day since this also encourages colour extraction. After about a week, the optimum colouring has been expressed (after this point a solution of harsh tannins

can develop). The fermenting pulp should then be squeezed through a cloth or press. The juice is then sweetened and fermentation proceeds as usual.

Further colour changes can occur during the period in the bottle. If the wines receive excessive exposure to oxygen during storage, the red tones turn to shades of brown.

Red wines can be light, full-bodied, dessert, long-storing and medium-storing.

The classification for the type of wine is given with the recipes.

Rosé wines

Rosé wines should have a fresh, fruity flavour, and because their modest alcohol content and traces of sugar make them susceptible to the growth of micro-organisms, they are not the easiest of wines for tation. Apple, elderflower, gooseberry, mead, white grape and white currant wines are probably best.

To test the dryness of the wine, make sure that the specific gravity is less than 1,000. You can also use a diabetic sugar tester, available from most chemists. Add one tablet to five drops of wine and ten of water. The colour indicates the amount of sugar present. Normally, 50 g (2 oz) sugar is needed for every 5 litres (1 gall) of completely dry wine. If, according to the test, the wine contains one-half per cent of sugar, then add 25 g (1 oz) sugar per 5 litres (1 gall) or *pro rata* for other concentrations. It is, perhaps, more convenient to add sugar to taste and then to make a test bottling. Fill a champagne bottle with the wine, wire down the cork and keep at 21°C (70°F) for a month, wrapped in a thick cloth, to see whether gas and a yeast deposit develop. If the cork is seen to be straining against the rim, gas formation has been excessive and the wine contains too much yeast and nutrients. Store the wine for another month and repeat the test. Eventually, the wine will develop sufficient gas without excessive gas and yeast deposit formation.

On the other hand, the wine may not be producing enough gas on the first test. Repeat after the addition of a champagne yeast and, if this does not solve the problem, add 1 mg thiamin per 5 litres (1 gall) together with 5 g (1/6 oz) ammonium sulphate per 5 litres (1 gall). If the wine is still too alcoholic, it must be diluted with at least one-tenth of its volume of water.

When the sample of wine produces a reasonable amount of gas with a firm deposit, treat the remainder of the wine in the same way. Then, keeping the wine stirred, fill the champagne bottles, cork and wire them.

For the first six months of storage, keep the bottles stored upside down at 21°C (70°F). This causes the yeast to carbonate the wine and the deposit

to settle on the end of the cork. Shake the bottles at intervals to encourage the deposit to slide down the walls of the bottle. Allow all the yeast deposit to collect inside the cork. After six months, lift the bottles one by one out of the crate. Loosen the cork, and when it flies out cover the neck of the bottle with your thumb.

The bottle can then be set upright and corked or you can immediately serve your own sparkling wine to your appreciative guests.

Flower wines

Once upon a time—a long time ago —perfumed wines were regarded as the apogee of taste and elegance.

older roses, not the modern hybrids and floribundas, that have the finest scent. If you are making marigold wine, be sure to gather your flower-heads when the sun is at its height. Legend has it that you are actually bottling sunshine and the aroma will be that much more delicious.

Our medieval ancestors attributed many virtues to these country wines. To the ones that we have already cited, dandelion may be added, which even modern medical men acknowledge as a great purifier of the blood and which also has useful diuretic qualities.

Fruit wines

The yield of juice is extremely small from most fruits when they are crushed and pressed through muslin or similar filters. This is because most fruits contain a mucilaginous material called pectin which retains the juice in the individual fruit cells.

It is therefore necessary either: to add a commercial pectin-destroy-ing enzyme, such as Pectozyme;
or to break down the tissues by heating the fruit to 70°C (160°F) for a short time before pressing;
or to soak the crushed fruit in warm water to allow the natural fruit enzymes to act on the pectin.

The last method is the one usually used domestically for extracting fruit juices. The raw material should not be boiled as this will kill the natural fruit enzymes and produce a hazy wine that may afterwards need treating.

When it is necessary to cook the fruit in an open pan of water, note the volume at the start, and add water to replace that lost in the process. Where a recipe stipulates 5 litres (1 gall) water initially, the addition of 1·4 kg (3 lb) sugar will increase this by another 1 litre (1½ pints).

In most recipes the wine-maker is told to add all the sugar in one batch. If extra time can be given to the wine-making, more certain results can be obtained by adding only one-third of the sugar recommended in

Alas, apart from country wines, this fashion has quite vanished. Our an-cestors believed that wine should tickle the nostrils as well as the palate. They frequently added scented herbs to their drinks to bring about the desired results.

English scented wines were deli-cate in perfume compared with their exotic eastern counterparts. The per-fumes reflected the countryside after a shower of rain. For many years these wines were made from the wild flowers which grew in such abundance in the unpolluted fields and hedgerows.

Rose petal wine has beautifully refined aromatic virtues, but it is the

the recipe. When the juice is in active fermentation add a second third and the last third approximately two weeks later.

Care should be exercised when making spiced wines. Use the form of spice recommended, suspended in the wine in a muslin bag for the correct time and never use powdered spices. Heavily spiced wines should always be treated as sweet and not as dry wines.

In some recipes no yeast is added since the fruits themselves contain sufficient.

Where there is insufficient yeast present, or if the yeast content has been destroyed by heat treatment in extracting the juice, some yeast must be added. A wine yeast is best (see Yeast chart), adding the amount recommended. Alternatively, one teaspoonful of compressed baker's or brewer's yeast may be added to each 5 litres (1 gall). Cream the yeast in a little of the juice before adding to the main bulk. If only liquid brewer's yeast or 'barm' is available, then add one tablespoon of this to each 5 litres (1 gall) juice.

Problems of wine-making

Ideally, if you make the correct choice of juice treatment, yeast strain and after-fermentation treatment, there should be no problems in making your own wines. But even the most experienced home wine-maker can run in to problems —seasonal variations in the composition of the raw materials, for example, can cause trouble.

Basically, likely problems come under four headings:
faulty fermentation
hazes and deposits
colour changes
peculiar flavours

Faulty fermentation
Fermentation can cease prematurely for several reasons. The yeast strain may be unsuitable, the fermenting temperature incorrect, the nutrient

30

supply inadequate or the osmotic pressure wrong. The yeast used is of immense importance to the winemaker. Different strains vary in their ability to withstand alcohol and to settle out at the end of fermentation. General purpose yeasts are suitable for most dry wines. Special yeasts should be used for such wines as sauternes and sherry. For high-alcohol wines strains of *Saccharamyces oviformis* are essential; without them fermentation is protracted and ends unsatisfactorily. Strains of these yeasts can be bought in shops that sell wine-maker's equipment.

The fermentation temperature is vital. Too low a temperature will depress the rate of fermentation. So, too, will temperatures that fluctuate up and down. Generally, for red wines the temperature should be around 21-25°C (70-77°F) and for white wines the temperature should be kept between 15-21°C (60-70°F).

The supply of nutrients is essential to successful wine-making, and their lack is probably the most frequent cause of stuck fermentation. Nearly all yeasts need at least one of the B-group vitamins to work successfully. The requirement for such vitamins varies with the temperature, the type of yeast and the raw materials being used.

When fermenting full-juice wines all that is required is a little thiamin. But for low fruit-content recipes it is necessary to add 125 g (4 oz) per 5 litres (1 gall) dried malt extract or 137 ml ($\frac{1}{4}$ pint) 5 litres (1 gall) grape concentrate. Alternatively, and more simply, yeast nutrients are sold as commercial products and the instructions on the package will tell you how much to add.

Yeast nutrients contain soluble nitrogenous compounds as well as the B-group vitamins and these are important in obtaining satisfactory yeast growth. As a rule of thumb, the more alcohol to be produced, the greater the amount of yeast growth necessary for rapid fermentation.

The most simple yeast nutrient is

1 mg thiamin hydrochloride and 2 g ammonium sulphate for every 5 litres (1 gall) of dry wine and 1 mg thiamin hydrochloride and 4 g ammonium sulphate for every 5 litres (1 gall) high alcohol dessert wines.

There are times when re-fermentation can start in the bottle or storage jar. Everyone has heard stories of wine-makers being awakened by the sound of exploding bottles. This can only happen with sweet wines. But if you follow exactly the instructions for stabilizing, it need never happen to you. One Campden tablet per 5 litres (1 gall) will give added assurance.

Some sundriesmen also sell a 'wine stabilizer' that contains sufficient potassium sorbate to give 200 ppm sorbic acid in the wine. While this gives some extra assurance with the SO_2, it does have a taste of its own which you must decide whether you like.

Hazes
If fermentation continues after the wine has been bottled, hazes and deposits are bound to form. The hazes should be noticeable before you bottle the wine.

The most common cause of haze formation is over-boiling the raw materials. When fruit or vegetables are boiled, a large amount of the pectin becomes soluble. Boiling also destroys many of the enzymes which act with the yeast enzymes to destroy the pectin during fermentation. Therefore, any juice or extract that is prepared by boiling must be treated with a commercial pectin-destroying enzyme. The amount added is usually 7-12 g ($\frac{1}{4}$-$\frac{1}{2}$ oz) per 5 litres (1 gall) but the exact dosage is given by the manufacturer. If this is not added, the wine will always remain opalescent.

Some fruits that are used as raw materials contain a large amount of pectin and even if being used unboiled, need to have pectin enzymes added in order to extract the juice; blackcurrants for example.

The presence of soluble protein

stir vigorously while heating to 50°C (120°F). Repeat the next day and the following day.

The amount of suspension added to the hazed wine can vary according to the degree of haziness. Carry out a trial on a number of 1-litre (1¾-pint) samples, adding from 1 to 10 ml of the suspension. Leave overnight and find out which is the least amount for maximum clearing and treat the bulk of the wine with the appropriate amount. Alternatively, just add 30 ml of suspension per 5 litres (1 fl oz per gall).

Hazes can also be caused by excessive oxidation at any stage in the wine-making process. This is best avoided by efficient sulphiting, fermenting under an air lock, storing the wine in filled containers and using only thoroughly clean equipment. Wine that has developed an oxidation haze can be treated by the addition of an absorbent called PVP, but this is a salvage operation and the wine becomes neutral in flavour, fit only for blending purposes.

Microbiological hazes can be caused by the growth of lactic acid bacteria. They give the wine a silky sheen when it is swirled in a glass and held up to the light. These bacteria are in fact beneficial in some wine as they reduce high acidity, but in low-acid wines they spoil the flavour and can sometimes produce a condition known as 'oiliness' or 'ropiness'. The wine then pours like lubricating oil, and because fine particulares are held in suspension, filtering is difficult. Oiliness can be treated with two Campden tablets per 5 litres (1 gall). If this does not 'fine' the wine, treat as follows:

Dissolve 15 g (½ oz) BP-quality tannic acid in 100 ml (½ pint) water and 15 g (½ oz) edible gelatine in another 100 ml (½ pint) boiling water, stirring vigorously until dissolved. To each 5 litres (1 gall) sulphited wine add 30 ml (1 fl oz) of the tannic acid solution. Mix thoroughly and then add the same amount of the gelatine solution. Leave in a cool place. When the

will also cause a haze to form if the wine is overchilled. Such hazes are usually observed first when a wine does not clarify naturally and filters slowly. A protein haze is distinguished from those caused by pectin by adding thrice its volume of methylated spirits to a small sample. Pectinous wines will precipitate a jelly; proteinous wines will not.

If you use fresh fruit for the juice, this haze is not too common, but if you use fruit juice concentrates which have not been specially prepared for wine-makers, your wines may be prone to protein haze. The easiest way to get rid of a protein haze is to add 2-3 g (1/10 oz) BP tannic acid per 5 litres (1 gall) wine.

Protein hazes can also be removed by using genuine Wyoming-grade

Bentonite. It clears even the most stubborn protein haze overnight. Bentonite is a clay and has to be suspended in water before it can be used. The usual dilution is 5 g per 100 ml (1 oz per pint).

There are three ways to prepare a 5 per cent suspension of Bentonite:
1 Put all the ingredients in an electric liquidizer and leave running for several minutes. Repeat if necessary.
2 Mix a small quantity of the water with the powder. Stir vigorously and add the water splash by splash until a uniform suspension is obtained. If necessary, pour the suspension through organdie and knead any lumps with the fingers while the organdie is held in the liquid suspension.
3 Put the ingredients in a beaker,

wine has cleared, siphon it off the deposit. The solutions of tannic acid and gelatine do not keep well, so it is more economical to make one batch and treat all hazy wines at the same time.

Any equipment that has come into contact with the oily wine should be cleaned and sterilized thoroughly. If you do not do this, the bacteria will persist and infect more wine in the future.

Colour changes
There are times when a wine will turn black or brown when poured into a glass or is otherwise exposed to the air. There are two causes of this. The first is an excess of oxidizing enzymes, the second is the catalytic activity of iron and copper.

Oxidizing enzymes may be the cause if over-ripe fruit has been used. The metals may have come from unsuitable equipment or from industrial grades of grape concentrate. The darkening process commences only upon exposure to air. Before you can find out how to treat the colour change, you must first determine which of these two causes has been responsible.

Pour some of the guilty wine into three glasses. Leave one alone, as control, add a crushed segment of a Campden tablet to the second, and a pinch of citric acid to the third.

The wine in the first glass will, of course, darken overnight as it has been exposed to the air. If the wine to which the Campden tablet has been added is still its original colour, then excess of oxidizing enzyme is responsible for the colour change, in which case, add one Campden tablet to each 5 litres (1 gall) of the rest of the wine to prevent future colour change. If the third glass of citrated wine has remained light, then the presence of iron or copper salts is responsible. The cure for this is to add 3 g to every 5 litres (1 oz to every 10 gall) as citric acid combines with iron and copper salts, so preventing the darkening process. The addition of the citric acid will

prevent colour change, but will not remove the unpleasant metallic taste. The iron can be removed by adding 10 g fresh wheat bran to every 5 litres (3 oz to every 10 gall) to the wine and leaving it in a filled container for three days. The iron combines with a constituent of the bran, and when this is strained off the metal is removed with it.

Nevertheless, as with all things, prevention is better than cure.

Peculiar flavours
There is no excuse for badly flavoured wine. The principles of wine-making have been known and understood for hundreds of years and if they are carefully followed, flavour disasters can be avoided. However, we do not live in an ideal world and there are times when we find that the wine that we have carefully made and matured does have a distinctly peculiar flavour.

The most obvious of all the 'off' flavours is the taint of vinegar. This is normally caused by the presence of acetic acid bacteria on rotten fruit. These produce sulphite-binding compounds from the sugar, so rendering ineffective the sulphite introduced in the Campden tablet. The bacteria survive and grow once yeast fermentation is complete and the drink is exposed to air.

Another source of acetic acid is a group of yeasts, *Hansenula* spp., which produce a compound of acetic acid and ethyl alcohol called ethyl acetate. It smells of vinegar but does not have the acid taste.

Both these sources of vinegar flavour can be avoided by rejecting inferior or dirty materials. Make sure that you use only good-quality raw materials and that you sulphite the pulp or juice adequately. In this way you should avoid any such unfortunate occurrence.

Once the wine has turned vinegary you cannot make it drinkable again unless you resulphite the wine by adding Campden tablets and then use it for blending. Or you can allow the wine to turn to vinegar.

There is another cause of acetification that takes place anaerobically, in the absence of air. Lactic acid bacteria usually convert L-malic acid into lactic acid and carbon dioxide. But if citric acid is introduced, they will produce a proportion of acetic acid in addition. This is most likely to occur in wines made from pears or citrus fruits, which naturally contain citric acid, or where citric acid has been used to adjust the acidity of the juice. In such a case, substitute malic acid for citric acid when adjusting the juice's acidity, and also add adequate sulphite to reduce the risk of bacterial activity.

Another unfortunate flavour that can occur is the smell of rotten eggs. This results from the formation of hydrogen sulphide (H_2S), produced by a combination of a juice constituent and the yeast strain. You can avoid this unpleasant smell by ensuring that the yeast strain you use does not produce H_2S. Your supplier will be able to guide you.

A yeasty flavour may occur in your wine if too much thiamin has been added or if the wine has been left in contact with the yeast deposit for too long.

A low-acid wine, inadequately sulphited, fermented slowly and exposed to air during storage can develop an unpleasant 'mousey' flavour. Only about 30 per cent of wine-drinkers are sensitive to the flavour, but they hate it. There is so far no curative treatment, only avoidance of the causative conditions.

Generally, however, if you use the best ingredients, rely on expert advice, follow instructions carefully and make sure that all your equipment is scrupulously clean, your wine should not suffer from any flavours other than those associated with the delights of drinking wine.

Wine tasting
How can you tell a good wine from a bad one? How can you compare your homemade product with wines

bought over off-licence counters?

For a start, do not buy a bottle of *Château Mouton Rothschild* and try to match its taste and bouquet with the first wine that you have made. If you must compare your produce with commercial wine, try a litre bottle of *vin ordinaire*. If you feel that your wine stands comparison, you are well on the way to success.

To appreciate a wine fully, it is essential to have a quiet, relaxed atmosphere, a comfortable temperature and freedom from any marked smells. You should not be smoking when tasting wine, or the whole object of the exercise—to assess aroma, taste, texture, flavour and clarity—will be lost.

Aroma is assessed by breathing air from over the wine across specially sensitive areas at the back of the nose. Once the movement of air ceases there is no smell. There are many thousands of aromas—some pleasant, some not. If your wine has developed a fragrance that is pleasing to the nose, congratulations!

It is a strange fact that although there are hundreds of thousands of different foods and drinks in the world, there are only four detectable taste components—sweetness, acidity, saltiness and bitterness. The taste buds that recognize the first three are on the front or edge of the tongue, but the buds that recognize bitterness are at the back of the tongue, so bitterness is the last part of the taste that you will sense.

Three other sensations apart from taste are apparent in the mouth.

Astringency or roughness is caused when excess tannin in the wine reacts with protein cells from the walls of the mouth. An excess of copper or iron in the wine will also cause an unpleasant astringency. Finally, the mouth will tell the taster what the texture of the wine is. Texture is a complex sensation made up of the amounts of sugar, alcohol, and the soluble solids in the wine. It is easy to describe the difference between an egg flip and a dry white wine, but between two types of dry white wine the differences can only be experienced.

Aroma and taste are but two of the imponderables of flavour. True appreciation of flavour comes with experience and, in fact, appreciation can be compounded with experience. A bottle of good, sparkling rosé wine first tasted on an idyllic summer's day will be a delight; when future rosé wines are tasted something of that memory will come back and add something to the 'flavour' of the wine.

Whereas true appreciation can only come with experience, the actual mechanics of judging a wine are fairly straightforward. First look at the bottle and ask yourself if the wine is clear and free from any deposit. When the cork has been removed, check whether there are any bubbles of carbon dioxide in it. Unless it is a sparkling wine, the less it is a sparkling wine, the presence of carbon dioxide bubbles is a fault. Does it pour well, or like lubricating oil? If it pours like oil, then the wine has been spoiled microbiologically. Is the colour fresh and lively? If it has darkened, the wine has been affected by excessive concentrations of iron and copper, or by oxidizing agents.

Cup the glass in your hand and swirl the wine round. This warms the wine and increases its aroma. Breathe in quickly at the mouth of the glass and then take a deeper breath to confirm the first impression. Does it smell vinegary, or like rotten eggs? If so, the wine has been

affected by acetic acid or by hydrogen sulphide. Or does it conjure up the fragrance of the fruits from which the wine was made? Does it make you want to sip it slowly and savour it gently?

Roll some of the wine round your mouth, swallow a little and spit the rest out. Does it please, or is there a metallic taste or a 'mousey' flavour?

Not only should there be an absence of all the faults mentioned, but also the taste balance of the wine must be satisfactory. No one quality should stand out above all the others. A dry white wine should not be excessively acid, or have more than just a suspicion of sweetness. No wine should be excessively astringent or bitter. A sweet wine should not be excessively sweet to the extent that sweetness is the only taste left on the palate. The amount of alcohol is vital—too little will make a wine characterless, too much will

overwhelm all other flavours.

A wine that is pleasant to begin with but which leaves no memory, no nutty after-taste and no sensation of mellowness, is a young wine of little consequence. But one which excites the mind, seduces the palate and leaves an underlying subtle impression of strength is a wine to be valued and stored in the mind as one of the joys of good living.

Storing and serving wine

Wine should always be stored in a dry, dark place. A cellar is the ideal situation, provided it is dry and that the temperature can be maintained at around 10-15°C (50-60°F). Few people have cellars today, so the best arrangement is to find a cool, dark corner to rack your wine.

A bottle of wine should always be stored on its side since it is essential

to keep the cork moist, otherwise oxygen can get into the wine through the cork.

Red wine should be served at room temperature. Open the bottle an hour or so before serving. This will allow the 'bouquet' to develop. It is also a good idea—but not really necessary—to decant red wine, but this must be done carefully because there tends to be sediment left at the bottom of the bottle. Careful decanting means this will be left in the bottle not served to your guests.

White wine does not really need decanting. Its sediment is harmless (for that matter, so is the sediment in red wine) and is also colourless, so your guests will almost certainly not notice it.

White wines should always be served chilled—and well chilled, too. Nothing is less tempting than 'warmish' white wine. Your bottle should be placed in the refrigerator

Container sizes

Bottles	Metric/in cl	Imperial/in fl oz
Miniature	2·8	1
Quarter	18·5	$6\frac{1}{2}$
Half	34	$13\frac{1}{3}$
Hock bottle	72	$25\frac{1}{2}$
Sauternes bottle	75	$26\frac{2}{3}$
Burgundy bottle	80	$28\frac{1}{2}$
Litre bottle	1 litre	$35\frac{1}{2}$
Large Chianti bottle	1·75 litre	63
Demijohn	4·8 litre	170

Large bottles/jars	in bottle equiv.	in imperial gallons
Magnum	2	$\frac{1}{3}$
Jeroboam	4	$\frac{2}{3}$
Rehoboam	6	1
Methuselah	8	$1\frac{1}{3}$
Salmanazar	12	2
Balthazar	16	$2\frac{2}{3}$
Nebuchadnezzar	20	$3\frac{1}{3}$

Wine casks	in bottle equiv.	in imperial gallons
Hogshead	315	$52\frac{1}{2}$
Butt	648	108
Pipe	690	115
Tun	1,260	210

Beer casks	in pint bottle equiv.	in imperial gallons
Pin	36	$4\frac{1}{2}$
Firkin	72	9
Kilderkin	144	18
Barrel	288	36

(not the freezing compartment) for about an hour before you serve it.

When pouring wine do *not* fill the glass—which should preferably be a clear glass with a generously-sized bowl—to the brim. There should be space at the top to allow the bouquet to be appreciated. Fill the glass about half to two-thirds full. You cannot, of course, instruct your guests on how to drink the wine, but we hope you take yours with the degree of care and appreciation that a good wine demands. Do not hold the glass by the bowl between both hands, as this will make the wine too warm. A wine glass should be held by its stem, and the wine gently swirled round the glass before you

begin to drink so that you get the full benefit of the wine's bouquet. A refined and appreciative sniff is not only permitted but is a necessity. Allow the wine to remain on the palate for a few seconds to enjoy the subtle flavour. If you are drinking someone else's wine this procedure is the best compliment you can pay.

There are two reasons for drinking: one is, when you are thirsty, to cure it; the other, when you are not thirsty, to prevent it.
Thomas Love Peacock (1785-1866)

The enemies of wine
Vinegar (acetic acid)   A French dressing of oil and vinegar served with salad will turn any wine drunk with it to acetic acid.

Citrus fruits (citric acid) The acid of lemons, limes, grapefruit and oranges will kill the taste of any wine.

Oily fish   Some oily fish will ruin the flavour of wine, especially red wine, giving it a metallic taste.

Wine with food and cooking with wine

Traditionally there are a few broad rules to follow when serving wines with meals. And this is one area where tradition is also good sense.

If you are preparing a large, formal dinner in which there will be an appropriate wine with every course, then remember that however many wines you are going to serve, a white wine should always come before a red except in the case of sweet dessert wines. A dry wine should precede a sweet one, and a young wine served before an old wine.

Fish should be accompanied by medium dry or dry white wines, and poultry with either a medium light red, a rosé or a white, but a fairly dry white.

Red wine goes with meat. The heavier, sweeter wines should be used with the dessert course.

When you are cooking with wine remember that it is the flavour of the wine and not its alcoholic content that you must consider. Do not overdo the wine. A dash is sufficient. The food should not be drenched.

Delicate foods such as chicken, fish and veal should be cooked with white wine, if you are using wine.

Cook your red meats—beef, lamb, game—with red wine. There are exceptions, as with any other broad rule, and these would include classic dishes such as *coq au vin* and *filet de sole* which should be prepared with red and not white wine.

If you have any wine left over after a meal, this can be used in the cooking of your next meal. Pour the leftover into a small bottle and cork it. White wine remainders should be kept in the refrigerator.

Beer and cider can also be used in cookery, although their use is more restricted than wine. Beer is splendid for marinating and is essential for the classic Welsh rabbit.

The secret of the recipe methods

Traditional recipes

The wine recipe section is presented in three parts. In the first section are included traditional methods of home wine-making. The specific instructions are given for each recipe, followed by an instruction to 'proceed according to the type of wine desired'. The types include: dry still wine; dry sparkling wine (two methods); sweet still wine (two methods); sweet sparkling wine. The instructions for the method of making each type of wine are conveniently grouped together.

Traditional recipes
Apple
Apple (spiced)
Blackberry
Damson
Dandelion
Elderberry
Elderberry and raisin
Elderflower
Mixed fruit
Pansy
Parsley
Pear
Plum
Rose petal
Sloe
Tea
Whortleberry

Common method recipes

The second section deals with common methods for making types of wines: light red table wine; early-drinking red dessert wine; full-bodied red table wine; light fawn table wine; desert fawn wine; un-oxidized light white table wine and full-bodied fawn table wine. The individual recipes are listed alphabetically, according to the main ingredient, and classified according to type. Once you have made your choice, follow the specific instructions that apply to the recipe and then turn to the common method, which applies to the type classification. If, for example, you have decided to make a light red table wine with damsons, follow the specific instructions on how to deal with the damsons and then turn to common method 1, which is applicable to all recipes in group 1.

Common method 1
Beetroot
Blackberry
Black grape
Bullace
Damson
Elderberry
Elderberry and damson
Loganberry
Plum
Raspberry
Sloe
Strawberry

Common method 2
Blackberry and banana
Elderberry and banana
Elderberry and currant
Elderberry and peach
Elderberry and raisin
Loganberry and banana
Raspberry and banana

Common method 3
Potato and banana
Potato and fig
Potato and peach
Potato and prune
Potato and raisin

Common method 4
Blackberry
Elderberry
Loganberry
Loganberry and raspberry
Raspberry

Common method 5
Apricot
Banana
Peach
Raisin

Common method 6
Apple
Pear

Common method 7
Bullace
Damson
Morello cherry
Sloe

Common method 8
Apricot
Peach

Grouped ingredient recipes

The third section is a mixture of different recipes and different types of wine, categorized by type of major ingredient. The berry wines include blackcurrant and white currant; the cereal wines, rice and barley; and the vegetable wines, rhubarb and lettuce. The recipes are listed alphabetically. Specific instructions are given for each recipe, and in some cases you will find the instruction to 'proceed according to the type of wine desired'. In this case, use the same methods as those employed in section one for traditional wine-making techniques.

Flower wines
Dandelion
Elderflower
Marigold
Pansy
Rose petal (1)
Rose petal (2)

Shoot and leaf wines
Oakleaf

Berry wines
Gooseberry
Mulberry
Rosehip
Rowanberry
White grape

Cereal wines
Barley
Maize
Rice

Vegetable wines
Lettuce

Parsnip
Rhubarb

Currant wines
Redcurrant

Stone fruit wines
Date or fig

Traditional recipes

All the wines in this section can be made by following the instructions given here. Some of the recipes have been improved by applying aspects of modern wine techniques.

Alternative methods are given for dry still wines, dry sparkling wines, sweet still wines and sweet sparkling wines. If you want to make sweet sparkling apple wine, follow the basic fermenting instructions and then turn to the paragraph which deals with sweet sparkling wine.

Fermentation Follow the instructions for preparing and yeasting the extract given in the recipe for the wine you have decided to make.

Pour the sweetened, yeasted liquid into a glass jar or clean cask until it is filled. Keep any surplus in a bottle for topping up the main bulk during fermentation. Stand the jar or cask on a tray in a warm room. Soon fermentation will start and froth will pour over the side of the container into the tray. When the froth ceases, remove the tray, clean the jar and insert an air lock or loosely fitting cork. Keep warm.

When gas bubbles are no longer formed, proceed according to the type of wine required.

1 Dry still wines Place the jar in a cool room for 14 days, then siphon, or rack, the partially clarified liquid with a rubber tube into a clean jar, taking care not to disturb the yeast deposit. Make sure the second jar (storage jar) is completely full when the cork is inserted, wax the top of the cork and store in a cold cellar for six months. Again rack off the clear liquid (it can also be filtered if required), bottle and cork firmly.

Store the bottles on their sides for at least another six months before sampling. Longer storage improves the wine.

2 Dry sparkling wines (1) Use heavy glass bottles. Two alternative methods of preparation are possible: The jar of fermented wine is kept in a cool cellar for 14 days and then filtered or passed through a jelly bag to clear it. The clarified wine is bottled, and before corking two large chopped raisins are added to each bottle. Cork, wire or tie down and store the bottles on their sides in the cellar for six months when the wine should be adequately carbonated.

3 Dry sparkling wines (2) The jar of fermented wine is kept as cold as possible for 14 days when it is siphoned or racked from the yeast deposit. For each 5 litres (1 gall) wine boil up 100 g (4 oz) sugar in 275 ml (½ pint) water, skimming until scum no longer forms. When cold add to the wine, mix well, bottle and cork. Tie or wire the corks tightly and store the bottles on their sides in the cellar for at least six months.

4 Sweet still wines (1) Two alternative methods of preparation are possible:
Instead of using the amount of sugar specified in the recipe, use 2·8 kg (6 lb). Allow to ferment as long as it will, then treat as detailed in 1. The disadvantage of this method is that the sweetness of the final wine cannot be controlled and may vary from sickly sweet to slightly sweet. Its only merits are that it involves minimum amount of effort and the wine will not ferment in the bottle.

5 Sweet still wines (2) Add 350 g (12 oz) sugar to each 5 litres (1 gall) fermented wine, stir until dissolved, re-insert the air lock and allow to ferment in a warm room once more. When gas no longer forms, taste the wine and if it is not sweet add 350 g (12 oz) sugar and re-ferment. This should be repeated until the sugar remains unfermented. Do not add nutrients to

these wines after fermentation.

6 Sweet sparkling wines Use heavy glass bottles. This type of wine is most difficult to prepare without elaborate machinery since it is difficult to strike a proper balance between the sugar content of the wine and the amount of carbon dioxide formed. The following method is probably the safest and easiest way to make such wines. Once fermentation is completed, remove the jar to a cold room for 14 days. Siphon the wine into a series of small clean jars. Make sure they are completely full when corked, wax the tops and store in a cold cellar.

The correct time to bottle must be determined by trial, as follows: about four months later, sweeten one of the jars at the rate of 225 g (8 oz) sugar per 5 litres (1 gall) wine. Fill a champagne bottle three-quarters full with this sweetened wine, cork and wire it strongly and keep it in a warm room for 14 days. If only a slight yeast deposit forms, together with a reasonable amount of gas, all the wine may be similarly sweetened and bottled, but in this case each bottle should only have a very small air space. If, however, a heavy deposit forms in the original bottle and the cork strains against the retaining wire, it is unsafe to bottle the rest. In this case, repeat with a further bottle of sweetened wine at the beginning and middle of each succeeding month until the wine can be carbonated safely. Then sweeten the remaining wine, bottle, cork, wire and store the bottles on their sides in the cellar for at least six months before sampling.

> **Sparkling wines**
> It is especially important when making sparkling wines to check constantly for signs of straining corks, which can indicate that the bottle is about to explode. At the first sign of a threatened explosion, remove the cork immediately.

Apple

1 kg (2 lb) white sugar
5 litres (1 gall) draught cider
25 g (1 oz) root ginger
1 stick cinnamon
500 g (1 lb) raisins, chopped
yeast (optional)

Dissolve the sugar in the cider and add the spices (in a muslin bag). Let it stand for four days in a bowl. Remove the spice bag, pour the liquid into a jar and add the raisins. Add the yeast, if necessary.

Proceed according to the type of wine desired.

Apple (spiced)

3 kg (6 lb) windfall apples
5 litres (1 gall) water
1·5 kg (3 lb) white sugar
1 lemon
15 g (½ oz) root ginger
yeast
225 g (8 oz) raisins, chopped

Cut the apples into very thin slices, and place in a bowl. Boil half the water, pour it over the apples and leave for two days, stirring at intervals. Strain through a thick cloth and pour the liquid into a jar. Return the pulp to the bowl. Boil the remaining water for half an hour with sugar, lemon rind and ginger, adding water to maintain the original volume. Pour this, while still boiling, over the pulp and leave for a further two days. Mash with a wooden spoon occasionally. Squeeze out through a thick cloth and add the second extract to the first. Discard the pulp. Add the yeast and chopped raisins.

Proceed according to the type of wine desired.

> Let us have wine and women,
> mirth and laughter,
> Sermons and soda-water the
> day after.
> **Lord Byron (1788-1824)**

Blackberry

15 g (½ oz) root ginger
2 lemons
6 cloves
5 litres (1 gall) water
2 kg (4 lb) white sugar
2 kg (4 lb) blackberries
yeast

Put the bruised ginger in a muslin bag with the lemon rind and cloves. Suspend the bag in the water. Add the sugar and boil for 30 minutes. Skim the surface and add water to maintain the original volume. Mash the ripe, dry berries and when the liquid has cooled, add the fruit. When cold, add the yeast and lemon juice and stand for two days, stirring twice each day. Squeeze through muslin.

Proceed according to the type of wine desired.

Damson (spiced)

2 kg (4 lb) damsons
5 litres (1 gall) water
15 g (½ oz) root ginger
2 lemons
yeast
1·5 kg (3 lb) white sugar

Bruise the damsons in a bowl and add the water, bruised ginger, lemon juice and grated rind (having removed the pith). Add the yeast and cover with a thick cloth. Allow the mixture to stand in a warm place for ten days, stirring each day. Strain the liquid through muslin and dissolve the sugar in the juice.

Proceed according to the type of wine desired.

Dandelion

5 litres (1 gall) dandelion heads
2 kg (4 lb) demerara sugar
5 litres (1 gall) water
225 g (8 oz) raisins, chopped
5 g (¼ oz) root ginger
1 orange
1 lemon
yeast

Measure the yellow dandelion heads into a pan and pour boiling water over them. Leave for three days, stirring several times each day. Strain into a pan and add the orange and lemon rind (having removed the pith), sugar and bruised ginger. Bring to the boil and simmer for 30 minutes, adding more water to maintain the original volume. Strain again. When cool add the yeast and the orange and lemon juice. Pour the liquid into a jar with the chopped raisins.

Proceed according to the type of wine desired. (Recommended as a sweet wine.)

Keep in the bottle for one year before sampling.

Dandelion

Although the dandelion is usually described as a 'pestiferous weed', it is at the same time a most useful plant.

The leaves are bitter and are sometimes eaten as a salad or cooked for pot herbs. They can also be used in place of mulberry leaves as a diet for silkworms.

The root, roasted and ground, can be used as a substitute for coffee.

Elderberry

1 kg (2 lb) elderberries
5 litres (1 gall) water
1 lemon
15 g (½ oz) root ginger
1 stick cinnamon
5 g (¼ oz) cloves
1·5 kg (3 lb) demerara sugar
yeast
225 g (8 oz) raisins, chopped

Remove the stalks from the elderberries and mash the fruit in a bowl. Boil the water and pour over the berries. Leave for two days, stirring daily. Strain through muslin. Slice the lemon and bruise the ginger. Put the ginger, lemon, cinnamon and cloves into a muslin bag. Boil the bag in 0·5 litre (1 pint) of the juice for 20 minutes. Remove the bag. When cool, add the spiced juice to the bulk. Dissolve the sugar in the juice. Add the yeast and chopped raisins.

Proceed according to the type of wine desired.

Elderberry and raisin

2·5 kg (6 lb) raisins, chopped
yeast
5 litres (1 gall) water
1 kg (2 lb) elderberries

Put the chopped raisins into a jar with the yeast. Pour in cold water. Insert an airlock or a loosely fitting cork and leave for 14 days, shaking the jar each day. After 14 days, remove the stalks from the elderberries and put the fruit into preserving jars. Heat in an oven at 130°C, 250°F/ Gas ½ until the juice runs from the fruit (usually this takes about 15 minutes). Strain through a sieve and add 0·5 litre (1 pint) cooled fruit juice to every 5 litres (1 gall) strained raisin juice.

Proceed according to the type of wine desired. (Recommended as a sweet still wine.)

Elderflower

0·5 litres (1 pint) elderflowers
2 lemons
1·5 kg (3 lb) white sugar
5 litres (1 gall) water
yeast

Gather the fully ripe flowerheads on a fine day. Rub together until there are sufficient florets to fill a 0·5-litre (1-pint) jug when gently pushed down. Place them in a bowl. Add the thinly pared and chopped rind (having removed the pith), lemon juice and sugar. Pour boiling water into the bowl. Stir until the sugar

dissolves. When cold, add yeast and leave until fermentation has lasted two days. Remove the florets by pouring through a coarse strainer.

Proceed according to the type of wine desired. (This makes a very good sparkling wine.)

Mixed fruit

500 g (1 lb) gooseberries
500 g (1 lb) blackcurrants
500 g (1 lb) redcurrants
500 g (1 lb) white currants
500 g (1 lb) strawberries
500 g (1 lb) raspberries
500 g (1 lb) black cherries
10 litres (2 gall) water
yeast
3 kg (6 lb) white sugar

Bruise the gooseberries in a bowl. Remove the stalks from the currants, strawberries and raspberries, mash them and add to the gooseberries. Stone and cut up the cherries and put them into the bowl. Add water and leave for two days, stirring twice each day. Add the yeast and sugar and stir until dissolved.

Proceed according to the type of wine desired.

Pansy

10 litres (2 gall) pansies
2 kg (4 lb) white sugar
15 g (½ oz) powdered ginger
nutrients
2 lemons
2 oranges
2 large sweet apples
5 litres (1 gall) water
yeast

Dry the freshly picked flowers in the sun for three days. When dry, alternately layer a bowl with pansies and sugar. Dust with ginger and nutrients. Leave for three days, stirring and mashing each day. Add the juice and thinly peeled rinds (having removed the pith) of the citrus fruit. Cut up the apples and add to the bowl along with luke-warm water. Add the yeast and leave for three

days, stirring vigorously twice each day. Strain.

Proceed according to the type of wine desired.

Parsley

500 g (1 lb) parsley heads
50 g (2 oz) mint
50 g (2 oz) mixed spring herbs
5 litres (1 gall) water
25 g (1 oz) root ginger
1 lemon
2 kg (4 lb) white sugar
nutrients
yeast

Wash and drain all the herbs and place them in a saucepan with water, bruised ginger and lemon rind (having removed the pith). Simmer for 45 minutes replacing any water that boils away. Strain and pour the hot liquid over the sugar and nutrients. Stir until dissolved. When cool, add the yeast and lemon juice.

Proceed according to the type of wine desired.

Pear (spiced)

3 kg (6 lb) windfall pears
5 litres (1 gall) water
1 lemon
15 g (½ oz) root ginger
1 kg (2 lb) white sugar
yeast
1 kg (2 lb) raisins, chopped

Slice the pears very thinly and put in a bowl. Boil half the water and pour over them. Add lemon juice. Leave for two days, stirring occasionally. Strain through a thick cloth and put the liquid into a jar. Return the pulp to the bowl. Boil the remaining water with the lemon pulp, ginger and sugar for half an hour, adding water to maintain the original volume. Pour the boiling mixture over the pear pulp and allow to stand for two days, mashing occasionally with wooden spoon. Squeeze through a thick cloth and add the liquid to the final extract. Discard the pulp. Add the yeast and chopped raisins.

Proceed according to the type of wine desired.

Plum

25 g (1 oz) root ginger
6 cloves
2 kg (4 lb) plums
1 lemon
1 orange
5 litres (1 gall) water
yeast
2 kg (4 lb) white sugar

Bruise the ginger in a bowl and add
the cloves. Cut up the plums, lemon
and orange and put in the bowl.
Boil the water and pour over the
fruit. Stand until cool and add the
yeast. Stand for five days, stirring
twice daily. Strain and dissolve the
sugar in the juice.
  Proceed according to the type of
wine desired.

Rose petal

5 litres (1 gall) rose petals
1·5 kg (3 lb) white sugar
nutrients
yeast
1 orange
1 lemon

Use strongly scented rose petals.
Dissolve the sugar in the water and
pour into a jar containing the rose
petals and nutrients. Add yeast and
fruit juices. Insert a loosely fitting
cork or cover the mouth with cling
wrap. Leave for nine days, shaking
once a day. Strain.
  Proceed according to the type of
wine desired.

Sloe

1 kg (2 lb) sloes
5 litres (1 gall) water
2 kg (4 lb) white sugar
yeast
25 g (1 oz) root ginger
2 chilli pods

Wash the sloes and remove the
stalks. Drain the fruit and put it into
a jug. Pour on boiling water. Leave
until the fruit bursts and then strain
through muslin. Dissolve the sugar

in the juice. When cool, add the yeast and bruised spices. Strain off the pulp after 14 days of fermentation.

Proceed according to the type of wine desired.

Tea

5 litres (1 gall) tea (own choice)
2 kg (4 lb) white sugar
4 lemons
yeast
500 g (1 lb) raisins, chopped

The best tea wine is made with leftovers from the pot. These should be kept in the refrigerator until the required amount has been collected. Add this to the sugar and lemon juice. Stir until the sugar dissolves. Add yeast and chopped raisins. Pour into a jar.

Proceed according to the type of wine desired.

Whortleberry

3 litres (5 pints) whortleberries
2·5 litres (4 pints) draught cider
50 g (2 oz) cream of tartar
2·5 litres (4 pints) water
1·5 kg (3½ lb) white sugar
25 g (1 oz) root ginger, bruised
5 ml (1 teaspoon) dried lavender
5 ml (1 teaspoon) rosemary leaves

Place all the ingredients in a jar. Insert an airlock or a loosely fitting cork, or cover the mouth of the jar with cling wrap. Leave in a warm room until gas is no longer formed. Strain through muslin.

Proceed according to the type of wine desired.

> *I always keep a supply of stimulant handy in case I see a snake—which I also keep handy.*
> **W. C. Fields (1880–1946)**

Common method 1

1 Place the fruit in a strong, plastic bag, large enough to contain at least 5 litres (1 gall) water.
2 Crush the Campden tablets and dissolve them in a little hot water.
3 Add the dissolved Campden tablets with the enzyme to the bag.
4 Squeeze the air out of the bag, tie the neck and place on a smooth surface.
5 Tread the bag until the fruit is crushed.
6 Support the bag in a carton (or bucket) and leave overnight.
7 On the next day, add 3·5 litres (6 pints) water to the bag.
8 Add the activated yeast culture to the bag.
9 Re-tie the bag loosely.
10 Store at a temperature of 24-27°C (75-80°F) for three days, squeezing the bag several times a day.
11 After three days, squeeze the juice through muslin into the fermenting vessel.
12 Dissolve the nutrients in a little water.
13 Add the dissolved nutrients and sugar to the vessel and bring the volume up to 5 litres (1 gall).
14 Seal tightly and keep at a temperature of 24-27°C (75-80°F) until gas production ceases and fermentation is complete.
15 Taste the wine. There should be no sensation of sweetness if all the sugar has been fermented. If the wine still tastes sweet, or has a specific gravity of over 1·000, treat as for 'stuck' wine.
16 Place the wine in the coldest part of the house.
17 Once the yeast has settled out, siphon the partially clear wine from above the yeast deposit into a suitably-sized container.
18 Keep as cold as possible. The wine should clarify completely if a moderately flocculent yeast has been used, otherwise it can be clarified after two months' storage with a filter bag and filter aid, or by treatment with Bentonite.
19 Siphon into bottles and cork.
46

20 Store the bottles at a temperature of 5-10°C (40-50°F) on their sides, if sealed with bark corks, otherwise, they can be kept upright.
Note For a sharper flavour, add either the juice of a lemon, malic or citric acid at the rate of 10 g per 5 litres (¼ oz per 1 gall) of juice.

Beetroot

classification light red table wine

2·5 kg (5 lb) beetroot
5 litres (1 gall) water
1·1 kg (2¼ lb) white sugar
3 Campden tablets
15 g (½ oz) pectin enzyme
15 g (½ oz) citric acid
nutrients
yeast

Clean the beetroot thoroughly and dice into small cubes. Boil 3·5 litres (6 pints) water, add the cubes of beetroot and simmer until they are just soft. Strain, and dissolve the Campden tablets, enzyme, acid and nutrients in the liquid. Leave overnight. The next day, add the yeast and store at a temperature of 24-27°C (75-80°F) for three days.
Follow **common method 1** from para. 11.
Note This wine is liable to precipitate pigment during storage, so drink while it is young.

Blackberry

classification light red table wine

500 g (1 lb) blackberries
3 Campden tablets
15 g (½ oz) pectin enzyme
5 litres (1 gall) water
yeast
nutrients
1·1 kg (2¼ lb) white sugar

Choose berries with an aromatic character and discard those from bushes which are tasteless or woody-flavoured. Wash the berries in cold water and drain in a colander.
Follow **common method 1**.

Black grape

classification light red table wine

2 kg (4 lb) black grapes
3 Campden tablets
15 g (½ oz) pectin enzyme
5 litres (1 gall) water
yeast
nutrients
1 kg (2¼ lb) white sugar

Pull the grapes from the strigs. Wash them thoroughly.
Follow **common method 1**.

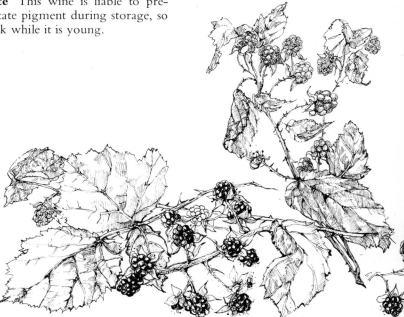

Bullace

classification light red table wine

1 kg (2 lb) bullaces
3 Campden tablets
15 g ($\frac{1}{2}$ oz) pectin enzyme
5 litres (1 gall) water
yeast
nutrients
1·1 kg (2$\frac{1}{4}$ lb) white sugar

Wash the fruit thoroughly. Pour 3·5 litres (6 pints) boiling water over the fruit to split the skins. Bring the mixture to the boil and allow to cool.

Follow **common method 1**.

Note Do not allow fermentation to take place on the pulp for longer than five days, otherwise the wine will acquire a flavour from the fruit kernel.

Beetroot

Aristotle, Pliny and Theophrastus all had a good word to say about the beetroot, which is a most useful plant.

It has a high sugar content and also contains a great many useful mineral salts. Its high iron content is useful for anaemia-sufferers. It is also a good digestive vegetable. If you have a sweet tooth, beetroot is one way of satisfying it without risk of putting on weight. Beetroot has a calorie count of 12 against 112 for sugar.

Elderberry (country method)

classification light red table wine

500 g (1 lb) elderberries
3 Campden tablets
15 g ($\frac{1}{2}$ oz) pectin enzyme
5 litres (1 gall) water
yeast
nutrients
1·1 kg (2$\frac{1}{4}$ lb) white sugar

Elderberries are best collected on a dry day when the birds are beginning to eat them. The best berries to collect are those on trees away from the roadside, as they are free from lead pollution caused by car exhaust contamination. Pick bunches with bright red stems and wash thoroughly. Pull the berries off with a large kitchen fork or an aluminium dog comb. Discard the bitter-flavoured stems.

Follow **common method 1**.

And Noah he often said to his wife, when he sat down to dine, 'I don't care where the water goes, if it doesn't get into the wine.'
G. K. Chesterton (1874-1936)

Elder

Many legends and superstitions surround the elder. In the Middle Ages it was commonly believed that the elder was the tree on which Judas hanged himself. It was also widely believed in some areas for several centuries that Christ's cross at the Crucifixion was made from elder wood. The Danes believed that the tree was under the special protection of the 'Elder Mother' and strict rules were applied by the superstitious in using the products of the tree. Flowers could not be gathered without the special permission of the 'Elder Mother' and the use of the wood for household furniture was taboo. Tradition had it that the 'Elder Mother' would strangle any baby unfortunate enough to be placed in an elder cradle.

The medicinal qualities of the elder were highly valued in the ancient world. The inner bark was used in Europe as a purgative. The strong, slightly sickly odour of the elder is believed to repel insects.

The flowers of the common elder are ready for picking in early summer and the berries ripen in the early autumn.

Let schoolmasters puzzle their brain,
With grammar, and nonsense, and learning,
Good liquor, I stoutly maintain,
Gives genius a better discerning.
Oliver Goldsmith (1730-74)

Elderberry and damson

classification light red table wine

1 kg (2 lb) damsons
500 g (1 lb) elderberries
3 Campden tablets
15 g ($\frac{1}{2}$ oz) pectin enzyme
5 litres (1 gall) water
yeast
nutrients
1·1 kg (2$\frac{1}{4}$ lb) white sugar

Wash the damsons. Pour 3·5 litres
(6 pints) boiling water over them to
split the skins. Bring the mixture to
the boil and allow to cool. Mean-
while, prepare the elderberries by
pulling the berries off with a large
kitchen fork or an aluminium dog
comb, discarding the bitter-flavoured stems. Add to the cooled
damson pulp.
　　Follow **common method 1**.

Loganberry

classification light red table wine

500 g (1 lb) loganberries
3 Campden tablets
15 g ($\frac{1}{2}$ oz) pectin enzyme
5 litres (1 gall) water
yeast
nutrients
1·1 kg (2$\frac{1}{4}$ lb) white sugar

Wash the fruit thoroughly.
　　Follow **common method 1**.

Raspberry

classification light red table wine

500 g (1 lb) raspberries
3 Campden tablets
15 g ($\frac{1}{2}$ oz) pectin enzyme
5 litres (1 gall) water
yeast
nutrients
1·1 kg (2$\frac{1}{4}$ lb) white sugar

Wash the fruit thoroughly.
　　Follow **common method 1**.

Damson

classification light red table wine

1 kg (2 lb) damsons
3 Campden tablets
15 g ($\frac{1}{2}$ oz) pectin enzyme
5 litres (1 gall) water
yeast
nutrients
1·1 kg (2$\frac{1}{4}$ lb) white sugar

Wash the fruit thoroughly. Pour 3·5 litres (6 pints) boiling water over the fruit to split the skins. Bring the mixture to the boil and allow to cool.
   Follow **common method 1**.
Note. Do not allow fermentation to take place on the pulp for longer than five days, otherwise the wine will acquire a flavour from the fruit kernel.

Strawberry

classification light red table wine

500 g (1 lb) strawberries
3 Campden tablets
15 g ($\frac{1}{2}$ oz) pectin enzyme
5 litres (1 gall) water
yeast
nutrients
1·1 kg (2$\frac{1}{4}$ lb) white sugar

Wash the strawberries thoroughly.
   Follow **common method 1**.
Note Strawberries do not give a deep colour and so are more suitable for making a rosé wine.

Plum

classification light red table wine

1 kg (2 lb) Victoria plums
3 Campden tablets
15 g ($\frac{1}{2}$ oz) pectin enzyme
5 litres (1 gall) water
yeast
nutrients
1·1 kg (2$\frac{1}{4}$ lb) white sugar

Wash the fruit thoroughly. Pour 3·5 litres (6 pints) boiling water over them to split the skins. Bring the mixture to the boil and allow to cool.
   Follow **common method 1**.
Note Do not allow fermentation to take place on the pulp for longer than five days, otherwise the wine will acquire a flavour from the fruit kernel.

Sloe

classification light red table wine

1 kg (2 lb) sloes
3 Campden tablets
15 g ($\frac{1}{2}$ oz) pectin enzyme
5 litres (1 gall) water
yeast
nutrients
1·1 kg (2$\frac{1}{4}$ lb) white sugar

Wash the sloes thoroughly. Pour 3·5 litres (6 pints) boiling water over them to split the skins. Bring the mixture to the boil and allow to cool.
   Follow **common method 1**.
Note Do not allow fermentation to take place on the pulp for longer than five days, otherwise the wine will acquire a flavour from the fruit kernel.

Plum

Plums are the most widely distributed of all stone fruits and in Europe plums are produced from Italy in the south to Norway and Sweden in the north. Yugoslavia bases its national liqueur, *Slivovica*, on the plum. Germany is also a great plum country and sometimes the German plum crop equals that of the USA. In Asia, Turkey and Japan are the main producers.
   Plums were planted in North America by the Pilgrim Fathers, in Massachusetts, and the French planted plums in Canada.

Common method 2

1 Dissolve 500 g (1 lb) sugar, Campden tablets, enzyme and nutrients in the combined fruit extract.
2 Add water to bring the volume up to 5 litres (1 gall).
3 On the next day, add the yeast.
4 Store for at least one week under an airlock, at a temperature of 25°C (77°F), until the rate of gas production slackens noticeably.
5 Test the specific gravity. When it is between 1·010 and 1·020, dissolve a further 100 g (4 oz) sugar in the wine.
6 Replace the airlock.
7 Keep the wine at the same temperature until gas production again slackens noticeably.
8 Add a further 100 g (4 oz) sugar to the wine, if necessary.
9 When fermentation ceases, put the wine in a cold place until clear.
10 Siphon it off from the yeast deposit into bottles and cork.
11 Keep the wine in a cool place for one month until it is ready to drink. If it is not sweet enough, add sugar to taste and keep under an airlock at 15°C (60°F) for at least three months. If, after three months, the wine is still not stable against fermentation, add more sugar and store for a further three months.

Blackberry and banana

classification early-drinking red dessert wine

1·5 kg (3 lb) dried bananas
1 kg (2 lb) blackberries
5 litres (1 gall) water
500 g (1 lb) white sugar
2 Campden tablets
15 g ($\frac{1}{2}$ oz) pectin enzyme
nutrients
yeast

Boil 1 litre (2 pints) water and pour over the bananas to extract the juice. When cool, strain water off, keeping it on one side. Chop the swollen bananas and pour a further 1 litre (2 pints) boiling water over them. When cool, strain water off and add the second amount to the first. Repeat a third time and discard the pulp. Add the third portion of water to the first two. Extract the juice of the blackberries by the double saucepan method. Add this juice to the banana extract.
Follow **common method 2**.

> The modern European blackberry is believed to owe its present form to the effects of the Ice Age. There is evidence that, at that time, two different species—the northern and southern varieties—were brought together by topographical changes. This was the origin of the hybridized European.

Elderberry and banana

classification early-drinking red dessert wine

1·5 kg (3 lb) dried bananas
1 kg (2 lb) elderberries
5 litres (1 gall) water
500 g (1 lb) white sugar
2 Campden tablets
15 g ($\frac{1}{2}$ oz) pectin enzyme
nutrients
yeast

Boil 1 litre (2 pints) water and pour over the bananas to extract the juice. When cool, strain water off, keeping it on one side. Chop the swollen bananas and pour a further 1 litre (2 pints) boiling water over them. When cool, strain water off and add the second amount to the first. Repeat a third time and discard the pulp. Add the third portion of liquid to the first two. Strig the elderberries and extract the juice by the double saucepan method. Add this juice to the banana extract.
Follow **common method 2**.

Elderberry and currant

classification early-drinking red dessert wine

1·5 kg (3 lb) currants
1 kg (2 lb) elderberries
5 litres (1 gall) water
500 g (1 lb) white sugar
2 Campden tablets
15 g ($\frac{1}{2}$ oz) pectin enzyme
nutrients
yeast

Wash the currants thoroughly. Boil 1 litre (2 pints) water and pour over the raisins. When cool, strain water off, keeping it on one side. Chop the currants and pour a further 1 litre (2 pints) boiling water over them. When cool, strain water off and add the second amount of liquid to the first. Repeat a third time and discard the pulp. Add the third portion of liquid to the first two. Strig the elderberries and extract juice. Add this juice to the currant extract.
    Follow **common method 2**.

Elderberry and peach

classification early-drinking red dessert wine.

1·5 kg (3 lb) peaches
1 kg (2 lb) elderberries
5 litres (1 gall) water
500 g (1 lb) white sugar
2 Campden tablets
15 g ($\frac{1}{2}$ oz) pectin enzyme
nutrients
yeast

Boil 1 litre (2 pints) water and pour over the peaches to extract the juice. When cool, strain water off, keeping it on one side. Chop the swollen peaches and pour a further 1 litre (2 pints) boiling water over them. When cool, strain water off and add the second amount to the first. Repeat a third time and discard the pulp. Add the third portion of liquid to the first two. Extract the juice of elderberries. Add this juice to the peach extract.
    Follow **common method 2**.

Elderberry and raisin

classification early-drinking red dessert wine

1·5 kg (3 lb) raisins
1 kg (2 lb) elderberries
5 litres (1 gall) water
500 g (1 lb) white sugar
2 Campden tablets
15 g ($\frac{1}{2}$ oz) pectin enzyme
nutrients
yeast

Wash the raisins thoroughly. Boil 1 litre (2 pints) water and pour over the raisins to extract the juice. When cool, strain the liquid off, keeping it on one side. Chop the swollen raisins and pour a further 1 litre (2 pints) boiling water over them. When cool, strain the liquid off and add the second amount of liquid to the first. Repeat a third time and discard the pulp. Add the third portion of liquid to the first two. Strig the elderberries and extract the juice by the double saucepan method. Add this juice to the raisin extract.
    Follow **common method 2**.

Peach

There are references to the fruit in Chinese writings of the fifth century BC. Greece and Rome became familiar with the peach just before the Christian era, and the Romans are believed to have taken it to countries throughout their empire. The early Spanish settlers took the peach to America, where it is known to have flourished in Mexico since AD 1600. There are thousands of varieties. About 89 per cent of the peach consists of water and, although it has fewer calories than either apples or pears and little protein, the yellow-fleshed peaches are very rich in Vitamin A.

Loganberry and banana

classification early-drinking red dessert wine

1·5 kg (3 lb) dried bananas
1 kg (2 lb) loganberries
5 litres (1 gall) water
500 g (1 lb) white sugar
2 Campden tablets
15 g ($\frac{1}{2}$ oz) pectin enzyme
nutrients
yeast

Boil 1 litre (2 pints) water and pour over the bananas to extract the juice. When cool, strain water off, keeping it on one side. Chop the swollen bananas and pour a further 1 litre (2 pints) boiling water over them. When cool, strain the liquid off and add the second amount to the first. Repeat a third time and discard the pulp. Add the third portion of liquid to the first two. Extract the juice of the loganberries. Add this juice to the banana extract.
    Follow **common method 2**.

Raspberry and banana

classification early-drinking red dessert wine

1·5 kg (3 lb) dried bananas
1 kg (2 lb) raspberries
5 litres (1 gall) water
500 g (1 lb) white sugar
2 Campden tablets
15 g ($\frac{1}{2}$ oz) pectin enzyme
nutrients
yeast

Boil 1 litre (2 pints) water and pour over the bananas to extract the juice. When cool, strain the liquid off, keeping it on one side. Chop the swollen bananas and pour a further 1 litre (2 pints) boiling water over them. When cool, strain the liquid off and add the second amount to the first. Repeat a third time and discard the pulp. Add the third portion of liquid to the first two. Extract the juice of raspberries. Add this juice to the banana extract.
    Follow **common method 2**.

Common method 3

1 When cool, add the yeast and allow to ferment at 21-24°C (70-75°F) under polythene film for one week.

2 Strain the juice through muslin into the fermenting vessel.

3 Add water to bring the volume up to 5 litres (1 gall).

4 Keep under an airlock.

5 When the wine tastes dry, add 225 g (8 oz) white sugar and replace airlock.

6 When fermentation ceases, sweeten the wine to taste and keep in a warm place for two months.

7 Should the wine ferment, add more sugar to sweeten until no gas is produced for two months.

8 Siphon the wine from above the yeast deposit into storage jars under a bung or airlock.

9 After three months, bottle the wine.

Note The wine will improve with storage but is rarely worth keeping after five years.

Potato and banana

classification dessert fawn wine

1 kg (2 lb) old potatoes
5 litres (1 gall) water
1 kg (2 lb) dried bananas
1 kg (2 lb) demerara sugar
500 g (1 lb) wheat
yeast
225 g (8 oz) white sugar
sugar to taste

Scrub the potatoes clean and chop them into 3.5 litres (6 pints) boiling water. Add the dried bananas, demerara sugar and wheat.

Follow **common method 3.**

> *I don't drink. I don't like it. It makes me feel good.*
> **Oscar Levant (Time, 5 May 1950)**

Potato and raisin

classification dessert fawn wine

1 kg (2 lb) old potatoes
5 litres (1 gall) water
1 kg (2 lb) raisins, chopped
1 kg (2 lb) demerara sugar
500 g (1 lb) wheat
yeast
225 g (8 oz) white sugar
sugar to taste

Scrub the potatoes clean and chop them into 3.5 litres (6 pints) boiling water. Add the chopped raisins, demerara sugar and wheat.

Follow **common method 3.**

Potato and peach

classification dessert fawn wine

1 kg (2 lb) old potatoes
5 litres (1 gall) water
1 kg (2 lb) dried peaches
1 kg (2 lb) demerara sugar
500 g (1 lb) wheat
yeast
225 g (8 oz) white sugar
sugar to taste

Scrub the potatoes clean and chop them into 3.5 litres (6 pints) boiling water. Add the dried peaches, demerara sugar and wheat.

Follow **common method 3.**

Potato and fig

classification dessert fawn wine

1 kg (2 lb) old potatoes
5 litres (1 gall) water
1 kg (2 lb) dried figs
1 kg (2 lb) demerara sugar
500 g (1 lb) wheat
yeast
225 g (8 oz) white sugar
sugar to taste

Scrub the potatoes clean and chop
them into 3·5 litres (6 pints) boiling
water. Add the dried figs, demerara
sugar and wheat.

Follow **common method 3**.

Potato and prune

classification dessert fawn wine

1 kg (2 lb) old potatoes
5 litres (1 gall) water
1 kg (2 lb) dried prunes
1 kg (2 lb) demerara sugar
500 g (1 lb) wheat
yeast
225 g (8 oz) white sugar
sugar to taste

Scrub the potatoes clean and chop
them into 3·5 litres (6 pints) boiling
water. Add the dried prunes,
demerara sugar and wheat.

Follow **common method 3**.

> **Potato**
> A potato tuber consists of
> anything from 10,000,000 to
> 100,000,000 tiny cells joined
> together by pectin, and the
> airspace between these tiny
> cells accounts for between
> one to two per cent of the
> tuber's total volume.

53

Common method 4

1 Wash the fruit in cold water and drain in a colander.
2 Place the fruit in a strong, plastic bag, large enough to contain at least 5 litres (1 gall) water.
3 Tie the neck tightly and tread the bag until the fruit is crushed.
4 Put the pulp into a fermenting vessel.
5 Crush the Campden tablets and dissolve them in a little hot water.
6 Add the dissolved Campden tablets with the enzyme to the vessel.
7 Mix thoroughly and leave overnight.
8 Add the yeast and cover with polythene film.
9 Mix two or three times a day for a week, by which time a rich red colour should be apparent.
10 Strain through muslin into the fermenting vessel and add the sugar.
11 Add water to bring the volume up to 5 litres (1 gall).
12 Fit the fermenting vessel with an airlock and keep at a temperature of 25°C (75°F) until fermentation ceases.
13 Taste the wine. If it is too sweet, treat as for 'stuck' wine.
14 Keep the wine in a cool place.
15 Once the yeast has settled out, siphon the wine from above the yeast deposit into storage jars, which must be filled and well sealed.
16 Store in a cool place for two years.
17 Taste the wine. It should have developed a dry, full-bodied and rich but not obtrusive flavour.
18 Siphon off into bottles, cork and store for one more year.

Note For a sharper flavour, add either the juice of a lemon, malic or citric acid at the rate of 10 g ($\frac{1}{4}$ oz) per 5 litres (1 gall) juice. Siphon off into bottles and cork. Store for one more year.

For a full-bodied red table wine that needs to be stored only for one year in the jar, and nine months to one year in the bottle, use 2·5 kg (5 lb) berries and 1·2 kg (2$\frac{1}{2}$ lb) white sugar.

Blackberry

classification full-bodied red table wine

5 kg (10 lb) blackberries
5 litres (1 gall) water
3 Campden tablets
15 g ($\frac{1}{2}$ oz) pectin enzyme
yeast
1 kg (2 lb) white sugar

Select the bushes from which you intend to gather the fruit with some care as flavour can vary from bush to bush. Do not pick berries which have a woody flavour or those which are tasteless. You need sweet, fragrant, plump berries.
Follow **common method 4.**

Elderberry

classification full-bodied red table wine

1·5 kg (3 lb) elderberries
5 litres (1 gall) water
3 Campden tablets
15 g ($\frac{1}{2}$ oz) pectin enzyme
yeast
1 kg (2 lb) white sugar

Follow **common method 4.**

Loganberry

classification full-bodied red table wine

2·5 kg (5 lb) loganberries
5 litres (1 gall) water
3 Campden tablets
15 g ($\frac{1}{2}$ oz) pectin enzyme
yeast
1·2 kg (2$\frac{1}{2}$ lb) white sugar

Follow **common method 4.**
Note Store in jars for one year, and in bottles for nine months.

> *If with water you fill up your glasses,*
> *You'll never write anything wise;*
> *For wine is the horse of Parnassus,*
> *Which hurries a bard to the skies.*
> **Thomas Moore (1779–1852)**

Loganberry and raspberry

classification full-bodied red table wine

1·2 kg (2½ lb) loganberries
1·2 kg (2½ lb) raspberries
5 litres (1 gall) water
3 Campden tablets
15 g (½ oz) pectin enzyme
yeast
1·2 kg (2½ lb) white sugar
    Follow **common method 4**.
Note Store in jars for one year, and in bottles for nine months.

Raspberry

classification full-bodied red table wine

2·5 kg (5 lb) raspberries
5 litres (1 gall) water
3 Campden tablets
15 g (½ oz) pectin enzyme
yeast
1·2 kg (2½ lb) white sugar

    Follow **common method 4**.
Note Store in jars for one year, and in bottles for nine months.

Common method 5

1 Boil 1·5 litres (3 pints) water and pour over the fruit.
2 When cool, strain the liquid off, keeping it on one side.
3 Chop up the swollen fruit.
4 Boil another 1·5 litres (3 pints) water and pour over the chopped fruit.
5 Mash the mixture while it is still warm.
6 Allow to cool, strain the liquid off and add the second amount to the first. Discard the pulp.
7 Put liquid into fermenting vessel.
8 Crush the Campden tablets and dissolve them in a little hot water.
9 Add the dissolved Campden tablets, enzyme, sugar and nutrients to the liquid. Add water to bring the volume up to 5 litres (1 gall).
10 Mix thoroughly and leave overnight.
11 Add the yeast and fit the fermenting vessel with an airlock until the wine tastes dry.
12 Store in a cold place until the wine becomes clear.
13 Siphon the wine from above the yeast deposit into storage jars. Store for six months. If it does not clear, siphon again, or treat with Bentonite.
14 Dissolve a Campden tablet in every 5 litres (1 gall) wine. Bottle.
Note The wine will be ready to drink after a few months' storage.

Apricot

classification light fawn table wine

500 g (1 lb) dried apricots
5 litres (1 gall) water
2 Campden tablets
15 g (½ oz) pectin enzyme
1 kg (2 lb) white sugar
nutrients
yeast

Follow **common method 5.**

Banana

classification light fawn table wine

500 g (1 lb) dried bananas
5 litres (1 gall) water
2 Campden tablets
15 g (½ oz) pectin enzyme
1 kg (2 lb) white sugar
nutrients
yeast

Follow **common method 5.**

Peach

classification light fawn table wine

500 g (1 lb) dried peaches
5 litres (1 gall) water
2 Campden tablets
15 g (½ oz) pectin enzyme
1 kg (2 lb) white sugar
nutrients
yeast

Follow **common method 5.**

> *Some men are like musical glasses: to produce their finest tones you must keep them wet.*
> **S. T. Coleridge (1772-1834)**

Common method 6

1 Put the fruit through a liquidizer. Alternatively, grate or slice it thinly.
2 Put the fruit into 3·5 litres (6 pints) water.
3 Crush the Campden tablets and dissolve them in a little hot water.
4 Add the dissolved Campden tablets with the enzyme to the fruit and water.
5 The next day, add the yeast.
6 Store for two or three days at a temperature of 18°C (65°F), mashing the pulp at intervals to liberate the juice.
7 Squeeze through muslin into the fermenting vessel.
8 Dissolve the sugar in the juice and add water to bring the volume up to 5 litres (1 gall).
9 Seal under an airlock and keep at a temperature of 18°C (65°F) until fermentation is complete.
10 Place the wine in a cool place.
11 Once the yeast has settled out, siphon the wine from above the yeast deposit into storage jars, which must be completely filled and well sealed. If further clarification is necessary, repeat the racking.
12 Dissolve one Campden tablet in every 5 litres (1 gall) wine when bottling. Store in a cool place for at least three months.

Raisin

classification   light fawn table wine

500 g (1 lb) raisins
5 litres (1 gall) water
2 Campden tablets
15 g ($\frac{1}{2}$ oz) pectin enzyme
1 kg (2 lb) white sugar
nutrients
yeast

Follow **common method 5.**

Apple

classification   unoxidized light white table wine

3 kg (6 lb) dessert apples
  or 2 kg (4 lb) cooking apples
5 litres (1 gall) water
2 Campden tablets
15 g ($\frac{1}{2}$ oz) pectin enzyme
yeast
1 kg (2 lb) white sugar

Follow **common method 6.**

Pear

classification   unoxidized light white table wine

2 kg (4 lb) dessert pears
1 kg (2 lb) Bramley seedling apples
5 litres (1 gall) water
3 Campden tablets
15 g ($\frac{1}{2}$ oz) pectin enzyme
yeast
1 kg (2 lb) white sugar

Follow **common method 6.**

Apple

Whether the apple originated in the garden of Eden or (as some scientists believe) in a region just south of the Caucasus is a source of speculation. Wherever it came from, the apple is today the most widely cultivated and the most popular fruit in the temperate zones of the world.

The Romans were great apple-eaters. As they made their way across Europe, they took the apple with them. Almost certainly, it was the Romans who introduced the apple into Britain.

Various kinds of apples were known and discussed in Europe more than 2,000 years ago. Cato, in the third century BC, listed seven popular varieties.

The early settlers in America were also devoted apple-eaters and large orchards were quickly developed. As early as 1759 Albemarle pippins were being exported from Virginia to England. Early traders and settlers took the apple to the southern hemisphere and to India, China and Japan. Europe still produces more than half of the world's apple crop.

Common method 7

1 Place the fruit in a strong plastic bag, large enough to contain at least 5 litres (1 gall) water.
2 Support the bag in a carton (or bucket).
3 Pour 3 litres (5 pints) boiling water over the fruit to split the skins, and allow to cool.
4 Crush the Campden tablets and dissolve them in a little hot water.
5 Add the dissolved Campden tablets and the enzyme to the bag.
6 Leave overnight.
7 On the next day, dissolve the sugar in the liquid, and add the yeast.
8 Leave for one week in the polythene bag, squeezing the bag several times a day. (Do not crush the stones.)
9 Squeeze the juice through muslin into the fermenting vessel.
10 Add water to bring the volume up to 5 litres (1 gall).
11 Fit the fermenting vessel with an airlock and keep at a temperature of 25°C (75°F) until fermentation ceases.
12 Once the yeast has settled out, siphon the wine from above the yeast deposit into storage jars.
13 Store in a cool place for two years.
14 Siphon off into bottles. Cork and store upright for another year.

Bullace

classification full-bodied red table wine

2 kg (4 lb) bullaces
5 litres (1 gall) water
2 Campden tablets
15 g (½ oz) pectin enzyme
1 kg (2 lb) white sugar
yeast

Wash the fruit thoroughly.
     Follow **common method 7.**

Cherry
Cherries fall into two broad groups, sweet and sour. The Morello cherry is the best-known of the sour varieties. Both the sweet dessert type and the sour culinary kind originated in Asia Minor.

Damson

classification full-bodied red table wine

2 kg (4 lb) damsons
5 litres (1 gall) water
2 Campden tablets
15 g (½ oz) pectin enzyme
1 kg (2 lb) white sugar
yeast

Wash the fruit thoroughly.
     Follow **common method 7.**

Morello cherry

classification full-bodied red table wine

2 kg (4 lb) Morello cherries
5 litres (1 gall) water
2 Campden tablets
15 g (½ oz) pectin enzyme
1 kg (2 lb) white sugar
yeast

Wash the fruit thoroughly. Nick a cross in one end of each cherry.
     Follow **common method 7.**

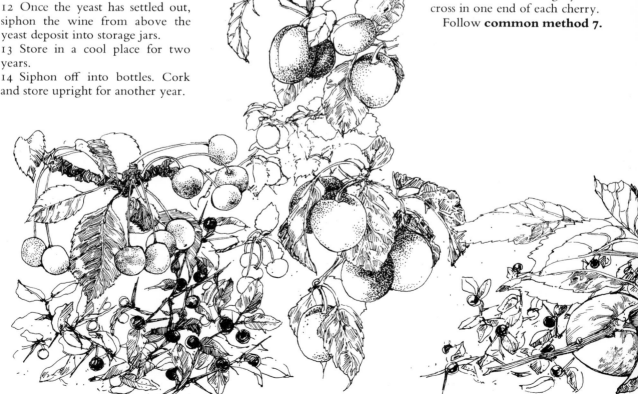

Sloe

classification full-bodied red table wine

2 kg (4 lb) sloes
5 litres (1 gall) water
2 Campden tablets
15 g (½ oz) pectin enzyme
1 kg (2 lb) white sugar
yeast

Wash the fruit thoroughly.
  Follow **common method 7.**

Common method 8

1 Boil 1·5 litres (3 pints) water and pour over the fruit to extract juice.
2 When cool, strain the liquid off, keeping it on one side.
3 Chop the swollen fruit.
4 Pour another 1·5 litres (3 pints) boiling water over it.
5 Crush the Campden tablets and dissolve in the first batch of liquid.
6 Add the chopped fruit and the second batch of liquid, when cool.
7 Add the enzyme and nutrients and allow to stand overnight.
8 On the next day, add the yeast.
9 Store under polythene film for three days or until fermentation starts.
10 Strain the juice through muslin into the fermenting vessel.
11 Dissolve the sugar in the liquid and add water to bring the volume up to 5 litres (1 gall).
12 Seal under an airlock until fermentation is complete.
13 Taste the wine. If it is not free of sugar, treat as for 'stuck' wine.
14 Store in a cool place.
15 Once the yeast has settled out, siphon the wine from above the yeast deposit into storage jars, which must be completely filled and well sealed.
16 Store for six months. Treat with Bentonite if still hazy.
17 Siphon off into bottles, seal and store for another three months.
Note This wine will keep for up to three years.

Apricot

classification full-bodied fawn table wine

500 g (1 lb) dried apricots
  or 1 kg (2 lb) fresh apricots
5 litres (1 gall) water
2 Campden tablets
15 g (½ oz) pectin enzyme
yeast
nutrients
1·5 kg (3 lb) white sugar

Follow **common method 8**.

Peach

classification full-bodied fawn table wine

500 g (1 lb) dried peaches
  or 1 kg (2 lb) fresh peaches
5 litres (1 gall) water
2 Campden tablets
15 g (½ oz) pectin enzyme
yeast
nutrients
1·5 kg (3 lb) white sugar

Follow **common method 8**.

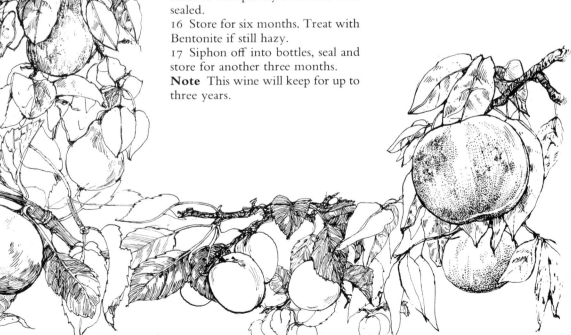

Flower wines

Dandelion

2·5 litres (4 pints) dandelion heads
5 litres (1 gall) water
4 oranges
yeast

Cut off the yellow heads of the dandelions, discarding the green portions. (Unless this is done, the wine will cease fermenting prematurely and cannot be restarted.) Boil the water and pour it over the flowers. Leave for two days. Peel the oranges thinly, removing the pith. Add the peel to the water and flowers. Boil the mixture for ten minutes. Strain mixture through muslin on to the sugar. When cool, halve all the oranges and squeeze the juice into the mixture. Add the yeast.

Proceed according to the type of wine desired (see page 39).

Elderflower (sparkling)

2 heads of elderflower
1 lemon
750 g (1½ lb) white sugar
30 ml (2 tablespoons) white wine
  vinegar
5 litres (1 gall) water

Pick the elderflower heads when they are in full bloom and put them into a bowl. Add lemon juice, rind (having removed the pith), sugar, vinegar and water. Leave for 24 hours and strain into strong, screw-topped bottles.
Note The wine should be sparkling and ready to drink after two weeks.

> There was a young lady of Kent,
> Who said that she knew what it meant
> When men asked her to dine,
> Gave her cocktails and wine,
> She knew what it meant, but she went.
> **Anon.**

Marigold

1·5 kg (3 lb) white sugar
5 litres (1 gall) water
5 litres (1 gall) marigold heads
2 lemons
yeast

Simmer the sugar and water for a few minutes to dissolve. When cool, add the crushed flowers (using the golden petals only), lemon juice and rind (having removed the pith). Add the yeast. Leave for four days, stirring twice daily. Strain.

Proceed according to the type of wine desired (see page 39).

Pansy

9 litres (2 gall) pansies
2 kg (4 lb) white sugar
15 g (½ oz) powdered ginger
2 lemons
2 oranges
2 large sweet apples, chopped
5 litres (1 gall) water
yeast

Put the freshly picked white or purple pansy flowers on a clean cloth and dry in the sun for three days. Layer the dried pansies and sugar in a bowl and dust with ginger. Leave for three days, stirring and mashing each day. Add the juice and rinds (having removed the pith) of the oranges and lemons, and the chopped apples. Warm the water and pour over the mixture. Add the

Note When making rose petal wine, use only the strongest-scented roses. The old-fashioned varieties, such as the China or musk rose, are suitable.

Rose petal 2

5 litres (1 gall) rose petals
1·5 kg (3 lb) white sugar
5 litres (1 gall) water
yeast
1 lemon
1 orange

Put the petals into a jar. Dissolve the sugar in the water and pour into the jar. Add the yeast and the juice of the orange and lemon. Insert a loosely fitting cork and leave for nine days, shaking each day. Strain.

Proceed according to the type of wine desired (see page 39).

Pansy
The pansy is one of the oldest of all our cultivated flowers. It has been grown in gardens for so long that its origins are no longer known.

One theory is that the common garden pansy is simply a cultivated form of *Viola tricolor*, which is a common weed in European grain fields.

The modern pansy is an artificial product and is very different from any related wild flower.

The pansy was a great favourite in Elizabethan times. Shakespeare wrote:
There's rosemary for
    remembrance
And·there is pansies, that's
    for thoughts.

What's drinking?
A mere pause from thinking.
Lord Byron (1788–1824)

This recipe has been modified from one written in the diary of an eighteenth-century Herefordshire farmer's wife. The original recommended generous additions of brandy and concluded, 'It be verrie strong and did make my head to busse and the chairs to dance so that I did go to my bedchamber and rest a while', which is why the brandy is no longer recommended.

Rose petal 1

2·5 litres (4 pints) rose petals
5 litres (1 gall) water
1·5 kg (3 lb) white sugar
yeast

Put the petals into a bowl. Boil 1 litre (2 pints) water and pour over the petals. Mash with a wooden spoon. When cool, strain, collecting the liquid in a jar. Return the petals to the bowl. Boil another 1 litre (2 pints) water and pour over the petals. Repeat mashing and straining process. Add the second batch of liquid to the first. Dissolve the sugar in the remaining 3 litres (4 pints) water and pour into the jar. Add the yeast.

Proceed according to the type of wine desired (see page 39).

yeast and leave for three days, stirring vigorously twice daily. Strain.

Proceed according to the type of wine desired (see page 39).

Shoot and leaf wines
Oak leaf

5 litres (1 gall) oak leaves
5 litres (1 gall) water
1·5 kg (4 lb) white sugar
1 lemon
3 sweet oranges
yeast

Pick the leaves during the last week of June or the first week in July. If the leaves are picked from trees in a town, wash thoroughly in cold water and drain. Boil the water and pour over the leaves. Leave for 24 hours. Strain off the leaves and simmer the liquid with the sugar and grated lemon rinds for 30 minutes. When cool, add the yeast and the juice of the fruit.

Proceed according to the type of wine desired (see page 39).

Berry wines
Gooseberry

2 kg (4 lb) gooseberries
5 litres (1 gall) water
1·5 kg (3 lb) white sugar
yeast

Pick the ripe gooseberries on a dry day. Choose large, juicy fruit. Put into a bowl. Boil the water and pour over the fruit. Allow to stand for two days, stirring twice a day. Squeeze the liquid through muslin, crushing the fruit with the flat end of a bottle. Dissolve the sugar in the liquid. Add the yeast.

Proceed according to the type of wine desired (see page 39).

Mulberry

3 kg (6 lb) mulberries
5 litres (1 gall) water
2 kg (4 lb) white sugar
yeast

Wash the fruit thoroughly, drain and place in a basin. Pour boiling water over the fruit. Allow to stand for two days, stirring well twice a day. Strain through muslin. Dissolve the sugar in the juice and add the yeast.

Proceed according to the type of wine desired (see page 39).

Rosehip

3 litres (4 pints) rosehips
5 litres (1 gall) water
3 Campden tablets
1·5 kg (3 lb) white sugar
2 oranges
1 lemon
15 g (½ oz) pectin enzyme
yeast

Crush the hips by hammering or putting under a garden roller. Put them into a bowl. Boil 3·5 litres (6 pints) water and pour over the hips. Allow to cool. Crush the Campden tablets and dissolve them in the liquid with the sugar. Peel the lemon, removing the pith. Add the lemon rind and the orange juice to the liquid. Leave overnight. On the next day, add the enzyme and the yeast. Allow to ferment for at least one week. Strain. Add water to bring the volume up to 5 litres (1 gall). Pour into a jar. Fit an airlock

and allow fermentation to continue to dryness. Chill the wine. When clear, siphon off from above the yeast deposit. Store in sealed jars for six months. Bottle and leave for three months before drinking.
Note This will produce a full-bodied fawn table wine.

Rowanberry

2 kg (4 lb) rowanberries
225 g (8 oz) raisins, chopped
5 litres (1 gall) water
nutrients
2 Campden tablets
5 g (¼ oz) pectin enzyme
1·3 kg (2¾ lb) white sugar
15 g (½ oz) root ginger
yeast
sugar to taste

Mash the strigged, ripe berries in a bowl. Add the chopped raisins and pour 1·5 litres (3 pints) boiling water over the fruit. When cool, dissolve the nutrients and Campden tablets in the liquid. Stir in the enzyme. Leave for two days, stirring the mixture occasionally. Strain through muslin. Boil the sugar and bruised ginger in a further 1·5 litres (3 pints) water for 20 minutes. Pour over the residue of strained rowanberries and raisins. When cool, strain and add to the first batch of liquid. Add yeast to the combined extracts and pour into a fermentation vessel. Add

water to bring the volume up to 5 litres (1 gall).

Proceed according to the type of wine desired (see page 39).

White grape

2 kg (4 lb) white grapes
3 Campden tablets
5 litres (1 gall) water
500 g (1 lb) white sugar
15 g ($\frac{1}{2}$ oz) pectin enzyme
yeast

Strig the grapes and wash them thoroughly. Extract the juice either by putting them in a polythene bag and treading them underfoot, or by straining them through muslin. Crush the Campden tablets and dissolve them in the juice. Add water to bring the volume up to 5 litres (1 gall). Measure the specific gravity and increase to 1·090 by adding sugar. Three-quarter fill the fermentation vessels with the sweetened liquid and add the enzyme. The next day, add the yeast. Allow fermentation to begin. When gas forms readily, pour the wine into a suitably-sized container. Fit an airlock. When fermentation has ceased, store the wine in a cold place to allow the yeast to settle out. Add one Campden tablet per 5 litres (1 gall). Filter and bottle. Store for at least six months in a cold place. The wine improves in flavour up to three years after which it begins to lose quality.
Note This will produce an unoxidized light white table wine.

Cereal wines
Barley

500 g (1 lb) old potatoes
1·5 kg (3 lb) white or demerara sugar
500 g (1 lb) pearl or chicken barley, crushed
500 g (1 lb) raisins, chopped
5 litres (1 gall) water
yeast

Scrub the potatoes, cut them up into small pieces and put them into a bowl. Add the sugar, crushed barley and chopped raisins. Pour boiling water over them and stir until the sugar is dissolved. When cool, add the yeast. Pour into a wide-mouthed 5-litre (1-gall) jar. There will be approximately 1 litre (2 pints) liquid left over which should be kept in a bottle and allowed to ferment along with the original jar. This can be used for topping up during fermentation or at the time of storage. Keep the filled jar and bottle on a tray in a warm room. Soon froth will form and the jar should be kept full so that the froth is forced out. When froth ceases to form, clean the jar, remove the tray and fit an airlock or loosely fitting cork. When gas production ceases, siphon the wine from above the yeast deposit, into a clean jar, which must be completely filled and well sealed. Keep in a cool place for several months. Siphon off the clear liquid. Bottle, cork, wire and store the bottles on their sides.

Maize

4 sweet oranges
1 lemon
750 g (1$\frac{1}{2}$ lb) crushed maize
2 kg (4$\frac{1}{2}$ lb) demerara sugar
500 g (1 lb) raisins, chopped
5 litres (1 gall) water
yeast

Squeeze the oranges and lemon and pour the juice into a jug. Chop the peel into thin slices (having removed the pith). Put the rinds, crushed maize, sugar and chopped raisins into the jug. Warm the water and pour into the jug. Stir until sugar is dissolved. When cool, add the yeast. Keep the jug covered with a thick cloth in a warm room for three weeks. Stir each day. At the end of this period, strain and bottle. Cork loosely and keep in a cool room until the wine clears. Pour or siphon the wine from above the yeast deposit into bottles. Cork tightly and wire. Store the bottles on their sides for at least a year before sampling.
Note This will produce a sweet wine.

Rice

1·5 kg (3 lb) rice
1·5 kg (3 lb) sugar
500 g (1 lb) raisins, chopped
5 litres (1 gall) water
yeast

Crush the rice. Put the crushed rice, sugar and chopped raisins into a jug. Add hot water and stir until the sugar is dissolved. When cool, add the yeast. Cover with a thick cloth and store in a warm room for 12 days, stirring occasionally during the first three days. On the last day, skim the surface and strain the mixture through fine muslin or cheesecloth. Store the liquid in a completely filled jar in a cool place for six months. Do not cork until gas production ceases. At the end of the storage period, filter or siphon the wine from above the yeast deposit into bottles.

Vegetable wines
Lettuce

1·2 kg (2½ lb) lettuce
5 litres (1 gall) water
1·6 kg (3½ lb) white sugar
1 lemon
1 orange
225 g (8 oz) raisins, chopped
500 ml (1 pint) wheat
yeast

Chop the lettuce. Boil it in the water for half an hour, maintaining the volume. Strain into a jug. Slice the fruit. Add the sugar, sliced fruit and chopped raisins to the jug. Stir vigorously. When cool, add the wheat and yeast.

Proceed according to the type of wine desired (see page 39).

Parsnip

1·5 kg (3 lb) parsnips
5 litres (1 gall) water
3 Campden tablets
1·2 kg (2½ lb) white sugar
8 g (⅓ oz) citric, malic or tartaric acid
nutrients
15 g (½ oz) pectin enzyme
yeast

Select mild-flavoured parsnips and store them outside for one week to allow the starch to convert into sugar. Scrub the vegetables and chop them into 5 litres (6 pints) boiling water. When a fork can easily be pushed into the parsnips, strain. Crush the Campden tablets. Dissolve the sugar, crushed Campden tablets and the acid in the warm liquid. When completely cool, add the enzyme and the nutrients. Leave for 24 hours. Add water to bring up the volume to 5 litres (1 gall). Add the yeast. Ferment under an airlock. When dry, chill to clarify. Siphon off from above the yeast deposit into bottles. Add one Campden tablet per 5 litres (1 gall). Bottle.
Note This will produce an un-oxidized light white table wine.

Rhubarb

2 kg (4 lb) rhubarb
2 Campden tablets
5 litres (1 gall) water
1·2 kg (2½ lb) white sugar
nutrients
yeast

Wash the rhubarb stalks thoroughly. Slice into a bowl. Crush the Campden tablets and dissolve in 3·5 litres (6 pints) cold water. Pour over the rhubarb. Leave for 48 hours, stirring at intervals. Strain through muslin into fermentation vessel, squeezing as little as possible. Dissolve the sugar and the nutrients in the liquid and bring the volume up to 5 litres (1 gall) by adding water. Add the yeast. Fit an airlock and ferment at 15°C (60°F) until gas production ceases. Siphon off from above the yeast deposit into storage jars, which should be filled right up. Fit a safety bung and store for several months. Add one Campden tablet per 5 litres (1 gall). Bottle.
Note This will produce an un-oxidized light white table wine.

Currant wines
Redcurrant

1·5 kg (3 lb) redcurrants
5 litres (1 gall) water
2 kg (4 lb) white sugar

Strig the redcurrants and mash them in a bowl. Add cold water. Allow to stand for five days, stirring daily. Strain the juice through muslin. Dissolve the sugar in the juice.

Alternatively, squeeze the fruit through a sieve into the water, add the sugar and stir until dissolved.

Proceed according to the type of wine desired (see page 39).
Note No yeast is needed for this method.

Stone fruit wines
Date (or fig)

1 kg (2 lb) dried dates (or figs)
225 g (8 oz) raisins
5 litres (1 gall) water
2 tangerines
yeast
225 g (8 oz) white sugar
500 g (1 lb) white honey
5 g (¼ oz) pectin enzyme (optional)
extra white sugar for sweetening (optional)

Wash the dried dates and raisins under hot, running water. Chop coarsely. Boil 1 litre (2 pints) water and pour over the fruit. Mash with a wooden spoon. When cool, strain through muslin, collecting the liquid in a bowl or jug. Boil another 1 litre (2 pints) water and pour over the fruit. Repeat the mashing and straining process. Add the second batch of liquid to the first. Repeat the whole process once again. Allow to cool. (If the cooled liquid is turbid with unsettled sediment, add enzyme.) Add the grated rind of the tangerines and the juice to the bowl. Add the yeast. Cover with a cloth and leave in a warm room for three days. Strain. Dissolve the sugar and honey in the liquid. Add water to bring the volume up to 5 litres (1 gall). Pour into fermentation vessel.

Proceed according to the type of wine desired (see page 39).
Note This recipe gives a rich-flavoured wine which improves considerably on prolonged storage. In some old recipes 225 ml (½ pint) brandy is added per 5 litres (1 gall) wine just before storage.

> The fig was one of the earliest trees to be cultivated by man. The tree in the garden of Eden was, according to medieval rabbinical teaching, a fig tree, Eve using a leaf to save her blushes after eating the fruit.

From the gods to us ...with love

Mankind has been brewing beer for many thousands of years. The ancient Egyptians dedicated their beer to Osiris, believing that all good things come from the gods. Cider has been made wherever the apple has flourished and perry wherever pears grow. Mead, the honey drink, provided the month-long merriment in Norse wedding festivities and so gave us our (shortened) 'honeymoon' habits. Here is a collection of traditional, country and personal drinks recipes for honeymoons, parties and all special occasions.

Introduction

I stuff my skin, so full within,
Of jolly good ale and old,
Back and side go bare, go bare,
Both foot and hand go cold:
But belly God send thee good ale
enough
Whether it be new or old.

This hymn to good ale comes from that roistering drama of the early sixteenth century, *Gammer Gurton's Needle*, and one can almost hear those cheerful worthies thumping out the chorus.

Today ale is synonymous with beer but it was not always so. Until the end of the seventeenth century, ale signified a brew made with malt, yeast and water alone. Beer, on the other hand, was a malt brew in which hops had also been used. Today the term ale is not applied to black beers (stout and porter) or to lager beer. Old English ale of the 'back and side go bare' variety was a very potent brew indeed and had no rival until the fifteenth century when European brewers introduced beer. However, in the rural areas of England the love of the old ale lingered on until well into the eighteenth century.

Nobody quite knows the precise nature of the earliest fermented drinks. Brewing seems to have started in Babylon, where barley grew wild. The experts now believe there is good evidence that beer was made from malted grain as long ago as 6000 BC in Mesopotamia. It was certainly well established by the fourth or fifth millenium BC and we have knowledge of the types of beer the Babylonians quaffed way back in 1800 BC. The ancient Egyptians were a little slow off the mark compared with the Babylonians and their brewing skills probably developed quite independently. However, once they had acquired the knack they were so impressed by the new drink that they concluded it must be a gift from the god Osiris (some said of his wife Isis, but they were probably early

66

feminists) and made suitable oblations out of gratitude. At any rate, beer was well established in ancient Egypt by the year 2000 BC and there is a possibility that several different types were brewed by the Egyptians at least 1,000 years before then. Indeed, beer became the national drink of Egypt, although it is difficult for us to associate the traditional British pint with those sharply featured, ascetic-looking characters familiar to us from ancient Egyptian relics. Beer certainly played an important part in Egyptian religious ceremonies and was dispensed with considerable largesse at public festivals. Rameses III, who thrived around 1225 BC, must have been a particularly congenial monarch for he is believed to have distributed a remarkable quantity of it—some 125,000 litres—during his reign—almost enough to form a minor tributary to the Nile.

Beer was also used medicinally,

beer is really climatic. Beer tended to thrive in lands where the climate did not encourage the vine to prosper.

In Britain, beer was well-established by Ango-Saxon times—like the apple and central heating, it was probably a legacy from the Romans. By the Middle Ages most large households brewed their own ale, a duty mainly entrusted to the womenfolk. It is to this feminine tradition that we owe the current terms of 'maltster' and 'brewster'— the feminine forms of malter and brewer. The monks, who excelled in the convivial art of beverage-making, proved excellent brewers. The strength of their best brews became legendary. Of course, beer-drinking was far safer in those days than drinking water, unless you were lucky enough to live by a fresh spring.

Flemish settlers in Britain introduced the natives to hops in the sixteenth century. Until then brewers had been using malted wheat, oats and barley as the basis of their beers, and had sweetened them with honey.

As the whole country drank large quantities of beer, its production in those days, before road and rail networks had been established, was localized. Small commercial breweries sprang up in almost every town and sizeable village. Local tastes differed and so local brews tended to be distinctive and to reflect those tastes.

The beer was transported by horse-drawn dray from the brewery to the inn and this is the origin of the term 'porter'—or one who transports porter. The name 'porter' can still be seen in the glasswork of many old pubs in Britain and Ireland.

Unfortunately this blissful state of localized production allied to local tastes could not last forever. A process of rationalization set in and the small breweries began to amalgamate as the national economic system developed.

Local tastes were catered for less and less, and standard varieties of

but it is not quite clear which maladies—apart from depression—it was supposed to remedy.

The introduction of hops into brewing is a genuine mystery, but it has been rumoured that the Hebrews learned about them during their Babylonian captivity in the eighth and ninth centuries BC. The Greeks learned about brewing from the Egyptians, but although they undoubtedly grew hops the evidence that they used them in brew-

ing is more slender. The Romans learned from the Greeks and so the knowledge spread through the Roman Empire to Spain and Gaul. A trail of brewing knowledge soon spread across civilized Europe.

The Northern Europeans knew all about brewing long before the Christian era although the Celtic and Teutonic beverages used a mix of corn and honey and so might more properly be described as mead. The real clue to the popularity of

beers were developed. Increasingly sophisticated techniques allowed the brewers to produce more beer for less cost, but at the cost of loss of flavour and individuality.

Some brewers clung to their independence and continued to brew by time-honoured methods. Some insisted that their beer should be drawn from the barrel by the old hand-pump method. Their products have always been eagerly sought by dedicated beer-drinkers.

It has always been possible for anyone prepared to spend a little time, effort and patience to brew their own beer to their own taste. In the past decade many thousands of people have chosen to do just that. The introduction of kits with which you simply mix sugar, dried yeast and water has made beer-making a popular and productive hobby. With only a little care, there is no need to suffer a succession of popping corks and exploding bottles when making beer at home.

Before looking at the theory and practice of beer-making, it is as well that you should know the difference between the several types of beer that can be brewed in your kitchen.
Barley wine is a heavy, sweet beer and is very alcoholic. It has a full flavour and is slightly more bitter than other brown beers.

Bitter should have a strong flavour of hops and a fairly high alcohol content. The beer can vary in colour from brew to brew but it must have a strong residual bitterness.

Brown ale can range in colour from amber to very dark brown. It is slightly less hopped than bitter and should have a residual sweetness which is gained by adding lactose. This is a form of milk sugar. It is not fermentable by normal brewing yeast and is used as a sweetener.

Indian pale ale is a bitter beer which tastes of hops and has just a trace of malt flavour. It should leave a clean, light taste on the palate.

Irish stout is a dark, bitter, full-flavoured beer. It should pour with a close-knit, creamy head.

Lager is a light-bodied and light-coloured beer with a delicate hop flavour. A special yeast is required to make lager, and it is best used with European hops. Lager needs more care than beer when brewed in the home.

Milk stout (or **sweet stout**) should be dark and sweet with a slightly bitter tang to it.

Oatmeal stout is somewhere between Irish and milk stout in flavour and sweetness. It has a special taste which comes from the oatmeal.

All of these basic beers are mixtures of malted grain, water, sugar, yeast and hops. It is also possible to make 'beers' with nettles, dandelions, parsnips and a whole range of other basic ingredients.

Large-scale beer-producers begin the brewing process by spreading

the grain on the floor of their malt houses and, by strictly controlling the temperature and moisture, forcing all the grains to germinate at the same time. When germination is complete, all the starch is converted into fermentable sugar known as maltose. As soon as this has happened the grain is dried. The malted grain is then ground and mixed with water to make a mash. It is kept warm in a large container and strained. This liquor is known as the wort and must be sterilized by boiling and cooling afterwards. Sugar and yeast are added to the wort and the sugar converted into alcohol during fermentation.

When fermentation is complete, the liquid, which is now beer, is filtered and put into large containers ready for bottling.

The home beer-maker has a choice. He can either buy concentrated liquid malt to which he has to add grain malt and fresh hops, or he can use fresh malted grains. The concentrated liquid malt gives the beer body and the other ingredients add colour and flavour. Or he can use concentrated hopped malt wort. Added sugar gives extra alcohol. A strong beer needs about 900 g (2 lb) total sugar content per 4·5 litres (1 gall) while a weaker beer should have about 450 g (1 lb). The total sugar content is contained in the malt extract plus any added sugar.

If the beer is to be made from fresh malted grains, these must first be crushed in a mincer, mixed with water, and treated with conditioning salts. The mixture should then be held at 66°C (150°F) for at least one hour to allow the conversion of the starch in the grain to malt sugar. You can tell when this has happened by dropping a little mash on to a white saucer, then adding half that amount of BP tincture. If the tincture turns blue, starch conversion has not yet been completed. When conversion is complete, the mash is strained, hops are added and the mixture is boiled. As the mixture cools, yeast is added. This yeast can be either top-fermenting (for most beers) or bottom-fermenting (for lagers). After fermentation, a little sugar is added and the beer is bottled.

The character of the water will play a part in determining the flavour of your beer. As a general guide, soft waters produce good brown ales and stouts, and hard water is ideal for the best bitter beers.

A third alternative is to use a beer kit. These kits, which should not be despised, are available at specialized shops, many chain chemists and department stores. They contain all the ingredients, except water, and provide clear instructions.

The inexperienced kit-user may have difficulty in establishing and maintaining a good, close-knit head on the beer. To counteract this problem, boil all the ingredients together and allow them to cool before adding the yeast. Also ensure that your kit has good fermenting yeast which minimizes this particular problem.

Ingredients

The ingredients for beer-making are not numerous. You will need:

Water

Ordinary tap water is normally used in the home production of beer. Hard and soft water are best suited to different types of beer. But you can soften hard water and harden soft water by adding chemicals to your local tap water. Any qualified chemist will tell you which chemicals you should use to produce the correct type of water for the beer you wish to make.

As a general rule, 5 ml (1 teaspoon) ordinary table salt added to 4·5 litres (1 gall) hard water will help when producing brown ales and stouts. If your tap water is soft, 5 ml (1 level teaspoon) magnesium sulphate added to each 4·5 litres (1 gall) brew will make the water suitable for bitters and pale ales. Suitable mixtures of conditioning salts can also be purchased.

Sugar

There is no reason why the amateur beermaker should not use ordinary granulated sugar. You can add a little brown sugar if you are making brown beers and stouts.

Malt extract

This can either be hopped or un-hopped. Hopped malt extract saves you the task of adding fresh hops. Some malt extracts are specially made to give the beer more body and good head retention.

Hops

To brew the best beer, use the best hops. These should be pale green or golden, depending on the type. Refuse to be palmed off with hops that are old and oxidized. If they have an excess of brown leaves, avoid them. The hops should have a clean fragrance. Avoid buying hops with a faint smell of cheese—they are past their best. Hops can be stored for some time in a sealed package in a cool, dry place.

Because hops lose some of their essential oils when they are boiled, some experts recommend keeping one-third of the total quantity aside until the last quarter of an hour of boiling. Others say that a few hops added before storage restores the balance.

Yeast

Always use a true strain of brewer's yeast—never baker's or wine yeast. Brewer's yeast ensures a better-quality drink, with all the yeast settled hard on the bottom (as long as you follow all the instructions. Bottom-fermenting yeast is used for brewing lager-type beer. This ferments for a longer time than other beers and at a temperature of 10-15°C (39-45°F). Top-fermenting yeast ferments at 18-23°C (58-60°F). If you allow the temperature to rise beyond these limits your brew may become too acrid. This is known as 'yeast bite'.

Barley

Many experts believe that barley is the earliest grain ever cultivated by man. It was first grown in Egypt, probably as long ago as 5000 BC. It was certainly used for beer-making in prehistoric times. Today nearly all beer is made from barley and no less than 10 per cent of the total estimated world barley is used for this purpose.

Hops

Cracked barley

70

Malt

Many people have quite the wrong impression of malt, associating it with the syrup substance which is really an extract of malt.

Properly speaking, malt is produced as the result of an enzymatic digestion. It is made by allowing cereal grains to germinate partially. This process modifies the seeds' natural substances.

Although any seed grain may be used, barley is the favourite grain. Some countries use rye, wheat or rice and some corn.

Most malt is used in brewing beer. About 9-22 kg (25-50 lb) malt is used to produce one barrel of beer, depending on the strength required.

Malt contains maltose, which is a sugar, dextrins and proteins and vitamins mainly of the B group.

Malting, brewing and baking are overlapping disciplines and have been known to man since long before recorded history. Under the Pharaohs of ancient Egypt the three allied skills developed into a triple industry. According to the Egyptians, Osiris, the god of light, health and agriculture, taught man to make malt as a first step to brewing a drink that would offset the worries and troubles that beset him in this world. Having been given this gift of malting knowledge, man was able to develop brewing.

The theory held today is that early man tasted the fermenting watery substance he found when stored grain became rain-soaked and developed the skill from that point after many trials and errors.

The ancients prepared their malt on a flat surface. They piled the grain about 60 cm (2 ft) high and watered it until rootlets appeared. This usually took about a couple of days. Early drying attempts, particularly in the hot climate of Egypt, probably relied on the sun.

These early processes continued for centuries. In Europe the monasteries and princely houses became the main brewers and developed the kiln-drying technique and the control of flavour.

Barley became the favoured grain. In Hamburg in the twelfth century, it was illegal to use any other grain for brewing.

Hand labour in the various malting processes continued to be the rule until well into the nineteenth century, when machinery was developed. Today most brewers buy their malt from large-scale malsters.

Glucose chippings

Yeast

Barley

Equipment

One vital point about equipment is to ensure that it is kept clean and sweet smelling. Dirty equipment will spoil your attempts to make good beer. Domestic detergents can be used, but if they fail to remove dirt, there are several products on the market which will clean your beer-making equipment. Cleanliness is essential.

Here is a list of the equipment you will need:

Large mashing vessel The larger size you use, the more beer you can brew at once.

Thermometer Ideally, this should be about 30 cm (12 in) long and should be suitable for immersing in hot liquid so that you can check the mashing temperature.

Plastic tubing Flexible 7-mm

($\frac{1}{4}$-in) tubing is necessary for siphoning off the beer into bottles. About 1 m (3 ft) should be enough.

Glass U-bend siphon tube If you fit this to the plastic tubing, it will prevent sediment being drawn up from the fermented beer.

Fermenting vessel A large plastic dustbin which holds about 22·5 litres (5 gall) is ideal. It should have a close-fitting lid and side handles

(for ease of lifting). It will be easier to keep clean if the inside is smooth.

Tap Fit this to the end of the tube that is filling the bottles to enable you to stop the flow of beer and to fill to a required level. If a small tap is not easily available, a clothes-peg will do almost as well.

Heat An ordinary gas or electric cooker is all that is required. Gas is slightly more efficient as it is easier to achieve instant heat control, but those who are used to cooking with electricity will have no difficulty in controlling the heat.

Bottles Beg, borrow or buy as many bottles as you need. They must be in good condition, neither cracked nor chipped. Do not use commercial non-retoppable bottles. The best bottles have screw tops. You can, of course, use corks to plug your bottles.

Hand crowner To close the corks.

Bottle brush To clean the insides of bottles thoroughly.

Plastic funnel

Large strainer

Long-handled wooden spoon

Measuring jug With either imperial or metric graduations.

Self-adhesive labels

Campden tablets These can be

used to sterilize your equipment. They produce a sterilizing agent (sulphur dioxide) when mixed with citric acid and dissolved in water. After you have washed your equipment, rinse it and·allow it to stand for a few minutes before use.

Hydrometer This allows you to measure the specific gravity of your brew. The hydrometer determines the amount of sugar in a given volume and from this you can calculate the potential amount of alcohol that the final brew would contain if fermentation were continued to the limit.

The weight of 28 cubic cm (1 cubic foot) of water at 15°C (60°F) is 28,349 g (1,000 oz) so the top of the graduated scale on the hydrometer is marked 1,000 after the Imperial measure. When the hydrometer floats in the water, it cuts it at this line. When sugar is added, the solution becomes thicker and the hydrometer floats with more of the neck sticking out. Generally speaking, the higher the specific gravity as shown on the hydrometer, the stronger the final brew will be. Thus by varying the amount of sugar and hence the specific gravity, you can vary the strength of your brews.

Do not be put off by the initial outlay involved in buying your equipment. It will pay handsome dividends in the form of cool, refreshing beers which you can drink with the satisfying knowledge that you have made them yourself.

Basic beer-making techniques

Having got your materials and equipment together, the next step is to make your beer. Below we give you, not a recipe for any particular beer, but a step-by-step guide to all the basic processes involved in beer-making. Individual recipes are given later.

The wort—from hopped malt extract

1 Open the can of malt extract.

2 Warm it by standing it in a saucepan of hot water (keep it hot on a low gas flame or electric heat) for about ten minutes.

3 Pour the contents of the can into a saucepan.

4 Add any extras specified in the recipe you are using.

5 Add the necessary water.

6 Stir to an even consistency.

7 Bring the mixture to the boil and boil fast for about five minutes.

8 While this is boiling, ensure that your fermenting vessel is scrupulously clean.

9 Pre-heat the fermenting vessel.

10 Measure out the necessary sugar and pour it into the fermenting vessel.

11 Add the contents of the saucepan, stirring well.

12 Bring wort up to required volume by adding cool water.

The wort—from malt and hops

1 Crush the malted grain in a cloth, with a rolling pin. After crushing, the husks should still be visible.

2 Mix the crushed grain with the required amount of hops and put the mixture in a clean muslin bag.

3 Place the bag of hops and malted grain in a covered saucepan with the necessary amount of water and bring to the boil.

4 Simmer for about 45 minutes.

5 If you have kept some hops aside to compensate for the loss which occurs in boiling, add them after 30 minutes.

7 Strain the contents in the fermenting vessel, having warmed the pot beforehand.

8 Bring the wort up to the required volume by adding cool water.

Fermentation

1 Take the temperature of the wort. Wait until it is about 15°C (60°F).
2 Sprinkle the yeast on to the surface of the wort and stir well.
3 Cover with a tight-fitting lid.
4 Ensure that the temperature of the room is warm and constant.
5 Stir the mixture five or six times during the first 24 hours.
6 Skim off any early yeasthead.
7 Give the wort one last stir and allow it to stand until the specific gravity is 1,000 (use a hydrometer to measure this).

The length of time fermentation takes depends very much on the room temperature in which the beer is being stored. The following general guide is useful:

    four days at 24°C (75°F)
    five days at 15°C (60°F)
    ten days at 10°C (50°F)

Bottling

This is the culmination of your efforts. To bottle successfully, you should follow this procedure:
1 Ensure the bottles you are going to use are completely sterile and that you have enough of them, as well as corks and stoppers.

2 Check that fermentation has stopped (when gas bubbles will be absent). Allow the brew to stand in a cool place for two or three days. Allow the sediment to settle.
3 Insert the glass U-bend tube into the plastic tubing and at the other end, attach the tap or close the tube with a clothes-peg.
4 Place the glass tube in the brew.
5 Turn on the tap (or take off the peg) and suck until the beer begins to flow.
6 Start to fill the bottles, turning the flow of beer on and off as required. This is easier if the bottles are about a foot lower than the vessel.
7 Add a little sugar to each bottle to produce more carbon dioxide, and so conditioned beer.
8 Screw the cap on tightly (or tap on the crown corks).
9 Label the bottles with the type of beer and the date of bottling.
10 Store in a warm place until secondary fermentation has finished.
11 After about two weeks, open one bottle and if there is an escape of gas, the beer is ready for final storage. Keep checking the beer in bottles all the time for signs of threatened explosion. If a cork

appears to be straining, remove the cork to allow the excess gas to escape. Try a bottle at intervals to ensure that accidental secondary fermentation is not taking place.
12 Store for the required time.
13 Drink it!

You may take your brew out of the fermenting vessel when it reaches a specific gravity of 1.000 and strain it off into 5-litre (1-gall) glass jars, sealed with an airlock. This will prevent bacterial infection. If you do this, allow the brew to reach its gravity of 1.000, and then let it stand for a few days until the sediment has settled. Then siphon off into bottles. If the first runnings of the beer are not clear, you can add beer-finings (available at some chemists and department stores), return the beer to the newly sterilized jars and allow it to stand for five to ten days. Then siphon it off.

Something can always go wrong even when the greatest care is taken. To help in those first frustrating moments when you cannot imagine what, if any, mistakes you have made, here is a list of common faults and hints on how to correct them.

Fault	Cause	Remedy
no fermentation	storage room too cold	raise the temperature to 15°C (60°F)
	poor yeast	do not use yeast more than twice and ensure that you are using brewer's or wine yeast as appropriate
	specific gravity too high	warm the brew and add more yeast or dilute with water
flat beer	bottles not firmly closed	ensure that corks are airtight
	left too long before bottling	decrease time between fermentation and bottling or add more sugar
	fermenting temperature too low	maintain temperatures at 15°C (60°F)
sour beer	equipment not sterile	use Campden tablets as directed
	yeast inactive	maintain better temperature control or change culture
too bitter	too many hops	use less
too sweet	too much malt	add 5 ml (1 teaspoon) from starter bottle
cloudy beer	storage temperature too high	remove to cooler place
	ineffective filtering	re-filter
	too little finings	add more

Recipes

Once you have studied all the instructions, hints and advice that have already been given. you should have no trouble making these brews.

Bitter

1·8 kg (4 lb) unhopped light malt extract
450 g (1 lb) cracked crystal malt
100 g (4 oz) hops
12 g ($\frac{1}{2}$ oz) dried yeast (top-fermenting)
900 g (2 lb) sugar
18 litres (4 gall) water

Stout

1·8 kg (4 lb) light malt extract
100 g (4 oz) cracked crystal malt (unhopped)
225 g (8 oz) black malt
75 g (3 oz) hops
12 g ($\frac{1}{2}$ oz) dried yeast
450 g (1 lb) sugar
13·5 litres (3 gall) water
7·5 ml (1$\frac{1}{2}$ level teaspoons) salt

Brown ale

1·8 kg (4 lb) unhopped light malt extract
325 g (12 oz) cracked crystal malt
100 g (4 oz) cracked roasted barley
75 g (3 oz) hops
12 g ($\frac{1}{2}$ oz) dried yeast
900 g (2 lb) sugar
18 litres (4 gall) water

Milk stout

450 g (1 lb) malt extract
100 g (4 oz) black malt grains
50 g (2 oz) flaked barley
37 g (1$\frac{1}{2}$ oz) hops
12 g ($\frac{1}{2}$ oz) dried yeast
7 g ($\frac{1}{4}$ oz) lactose
450 g (1 lb) brown sugar
22·5 litres (5 gall) water

Barley wine

1·8 kg (4 lb) unhopped malt extract
225 g (8 oz) cracked crystal malt
37 g (1$\frac{1}{2}$ oz) hops
7 g ($\frac{1}{4}$ oz) dried yeast
450 g (1 lb) sugar
9 litres (2 gall) water

You will need to stir the wort during fermentation to ensure that the sugar is fermented sufficiently. You will also find that it takes longer for the specific gravity to drop to the level necessary for bottling.

Lager

1·8 kg (4 lb) unhopped malt extract
100 g (4 oz) cracked malt extract
50 g (2 oz) hops
7 g ($\frac{1}{4}$ oz) dried yeast
450 g (1 lb) sugar
18 litres (4 gall) water

For successful lager-making, the brew should ferment at a temperature of 10°C (50°F). Once the beer is ready, keep it in the refrigerator. Few drinks are more delicious than ice-cold lager on a hot, summer's day.

Legal warning

In the UK, beer is subject to the same laws that govern the sale of homemade wines. No beer made at home may be sold or given away for sale unless the maker has a licence from HM Customs and Excise. Any breach of this law can lead to fines and/or imprisonment.

Readers outside the UK should check their own national laws.

Simple malt extract beer

500 g (1 lb) malt extract
500 g (1 lb) sugar (brown or white)
15 g (½ oz) hops
5 litres (1 gall) water
top-fermenting yeast

Boil the malt extract, hops, sugar and 2·5 litres (½ gall) water for one hour. If the mixture reduces, add water to bring it back to the original volume. Strain the brew through a muslin into a jug. When cool, make up the volume with 5 litres (1 gall) water and yeast. Skim off the first yeast head and discard it. Cover the container and leave it in a warm place until fermentation is completed. Gather the bottles together and make sure that they are thoroughly clean. Put a little sugar into each bottle and siphon the beer into them, leaving the yeast behind. Cork the bottles. The beer is ready for consumption as soon as secondary fermentation is completed.

Hops
The hop is an extremely vigorous plant—so vigorous that under good conditions it has been observed to grow 15 cm (6 in) or even more within the space of 24 hours. Its roots plunge down to a depth of 4·5 m (15 ft). Incidentally, like bath water, these stems always twine in a clockwise direction.

Less alcoholic simple malt beer

750 g (1½ lb) malt extract
3 litres (5 pints) water
25 g (1 oz) hops
powdered Irish moss
or proprietary finings
top-fermenting yeast
25 g (1 oz) white sugar

Dissolve the malt extract in 3 litres (5 pints) hot water, in a saucepan. Add the hops and the amount of Irish moss or finings as recommended by the manufacturer. Boil together for one hour. Allow the mixture to stand for one hour and then strain it through a stainless steel or heat-resistant plastic mesh. Re-strain it through the hops to assist clarification. Make the volume up to 5 litres (1 gall) by adding sufficient water. When the temperature is at 21-27°C (70-80°F) add the yeast. Maintain the temperature for two to four days when the specific gravity should have dropped to 1·010. Pour the liquid into a plastic barrel with the sugar. The beer is ready after a few days and does not need to be bottled. It can be run off the barrel under the pressure generated from the sugar priming. Eventually, however, you will have to pierce the bung hole and insert a small airlock.

Classical malted grain beer

100 g (4 oz) wheat flour
2 litres (3½ pints) water
100 g (4 oz) malt extract
100 g (4 oz) cracked crystal malt
15 g (½ oz) hops
top-fermenting yeast
225 g (8 oz) invert or brewing sugar

Make a paste with the wheat flour and a little water. Disperse this in 2 litres (3½ pints) water at a temperature of 66°C (150°F). Add proprietary salts if you live in a soft-water area. Dissolve the malt extract in the liquid. Ensure that the crystal malt is thoroughly cracked, and add to the mixture. Put the mixture into a bucket and maintain at 66°C (150°F) until all the starch has been converted into sugar.

To test this, take a drop from the bucket and place it in a saucer. Add a drop of iodine and if the iodine no longer turns blue the process has been completed.

Stir occasionally while waiting for the completion of the conversion. Add the hops and boil for about 30 minutes. Strain the mixture on to the invert sugar. Spray the residue with a fine spray of hot water and use these washings to make the final volume up to 5 litres (1 gall).

Pour into a fermenting vessel and when the temperature drops to 21-27°C (70-80°F) add the yeast. Remove the first yeast head and discard. Mix the contents of the vessel twice a day until a firm yeast head has been formed. When the specific gravity reaches 1·010, siphon off into an air-locked glass jar. When the specific gravity has reached 1·000, siphon off from the yeast deposit into bottles, into each of which a cube of sugar has been inserted. The beer is ready after about ten days.

Note As an alternative you can use 325 g (12 oz) malt extract and 100 g (4 oz) flaked barley instead of the first three ingredients.

True beer

5 litres (1 gall) water
750 g (1½ lb) pale malt, crushed
40 g (1½ oz) crystal malt, crushed
225 g (8 oz) brewing sugar
15 g (½ oz) Golding hops
top-fermenting yeast
dry beer finings

Heat 1·5 litres (2½ pints) water in an enamelled bucket to 77°C (170°F). Add proprietary salts if you live in a soft-water area.

Pour in the crushed malts, mixing slowly all the time. By the time this is completed, the temperature should have dropped to about 66°C (150°F). Place the brew in the oven pre-heated to 100°C, 200°F/Gas ¼.

Leave for two hours and then carry out the iodine test to ensure that the sugar conversion is complete. Pour the mixture through a strainer and spray the residue with 2·5 litres (4 pints) hot water.

Dissolve the brewing sugar in the combined hot liquids and bring the volume up to 5 litres (1 gall). Add hops and simmer gently for 2 hours, strain, adjust volume to 5 litres (1 gall), cool to 21°C (70°F) and add the yeast. Skim off the first head and allow to ferment to specific gravity 1·010. Skim off the second yeast head. This can be retained for future brewings. Siphon the beer into a plastic barrel and add 20 ml (4 teaspoons) sugar and the advised amount of finings. Leave for seven days after which the beer should be conditioned.

If you wish to bottle this beer, omit the finings and add 2·5 ml (½ teaspoon) sugar to each bottle and leave for five weeks.

True stout

500 g (1 lb) pale malt, crushed
100 g (4 oz) black malt, crushed
100 g (4 oz) flaked barley
100 g (4 oz) crystal malt, crushed
15 g (½ oz) hops
175 g (6 oz) brewing sugar

Use fresh malted grain method.

> *Good ale, the true and proper drink of Englishmen. He is not deserving of the name of Englishman, who speaketh against ale, that is good ale.*
> **George Borrow (1803–81)**

Dandelion beer

225 g (8 oz) dandelion plants
5 litres (1 gall) water
15 g (½ oz) root ginger
1 lemon
500 g (1 lb) demerara sugar
25 g (1 oz) cream of tartar
top-fermenting yeast

Dig up complete dandelions in the spring and wash them well. Cut off the thin fibrous roots and boil them in water with the bruised ginger and thinly peeled lemon rind for ten minutes. Strain and pour the hot liquid on to the sugar and cream of tartar. Stir until dissolved. When the liquid has cooled, add the yeast and the lemon juice and make the volume up to 5 litres (1 gall). Keep covered for three days to allow for active fermentation. Strain and bottle in *strong* screw-top or crown-corked bottles. Open a bottle at weekly intervals to test for adequate but not excessive gas pressure.

Ginger beer

25 g (1 oz) root ginger
15 g (½ oz) cream of tartar
1 lemon
5 litres (1 gall) water
500 g (1 lb) white sugar
top-fermenting yeast

Pour the bruised ginger, cream of tartar and thin lemon rind in a bowl. Cover with boiling water. Add the sugar and stir vigorously until the sugar has dissolved. Allow to cool. Add the yeast and the lemon juice and make up the volume to 5 litres (1 gall). Cover with a thick cloth and leave in a warm room until fermentation starts. Remove the scum. Siphon off the liquid without disturbing the yeast deposit. Bottle and cork as soon as possible. The beer is ready to drink as soon as it is charged with carbon dioxide. Drink soon!

Nettle beer 1

1 kg (2 lb) young nettles
5 litres (1 gall) water
2 lemons
500 g (1 lb) demerara sugar
25 g (1 oz) cream of tartar
top-fermenting yeast

Cut off and discard the nettle roots. Rinse the tops, drain and boil them in 4 litres (6 pints) water. Strain into a fermenting vessel containing the thinly peeled lemon rind, lemon juice, sugar and cream of tartar. Make up the volume to 5 litres (1 gall). Stir vigorously, and when cool add yeast. Cover and keep in a warm room. Allow three days for fermentation to take place. Strain and bottle. The beer should be ready after one week.

Nettle beer 2

5 litres (1 gall) fresh nettle tops
225 g (8 oz) malt extract
15 g (½ oz) root ginger
25 g (1 oz) hops
5 litres (1 gall) water
225 g (8 oz) white sugar
top-fermenting yeast

Boil all the ingredients, except the sugar and yeast, with 2·5 litres (½ gall) water, for one hour. Strain over the sugar into the fermenting vessel and bring the volume up to 5 litres (1 gall). Add the yeast and cover. Keep covered for three days in a warm place. When fermentation has taken place, strain and bottle.

What two ideas are more inseparable than Beer and Britannia?
Rev. Sydney Smith (1771–1845)

Cider

Cider is the fermented juice of apples which have been minced and pressed out in a fruit press.

From a mythological point of view, cider has the most respectable origins, or at any rate the apple from which it is derived has. Even if we draw a veil over that unfortunate episode in the Garden of Eden, we have the Greek legend in which the apple figures as 'the apple of discord'. Although the Golden Apples of the Hesperides sound marvellously evocative, it is now believed that they were oranges. The lissome and lively Atalanta offered to marry anyone who could out-run her. Hippomenes hit upon the bright idea of dropping three of the golden apples in her path. He had been given them by Aphrodite, the goddess of love, with just this seductive sort of purpose in mind. Atalanta stooped to pick one up and so lost the race to Hippomenes (loud laughter among the gods). Hippomenes and Atalanta, although blessed with a son, proved ungrateful to Aphrodite and were eventually turned into lions. Heracles was very partial to apples and the faithful placed apples on his shrine.

The Druids worshipped the apple tree, along with the oak, for one very good reason—the apple and the oak were the only trees in Britain on which their sacred mistletoe would grow.

It is also fascinating to note that, when Christianity established itself in Britain, it is supposed to have started off on the Isle of Avalon in Somersetshire—and Avalon meant 'Island of apples'.

The apple has long since lost all its sacred and mythological associations and although apples continue to thrive on Avalon, they are more likely to be cider apples.

However, all sorts of ceremonies connected with the apple did survive until quite recent times, such as pouring cider on to the soil of orchards at Christmas or on Twelfth Night. There was also 'bobbing' for

82

apples at Halloween, and the Saxons, incidentally, developed a habit of popping a roasted apple into their wassail bowl to improve the flavour.

Any variety of apple, including windfall fruit, can be used to make cider, but the best-quality drink is made using the true cider apples of south-east England. Cultivators such as Kingston Blacks, Foxwhelp, Crimson King and Langworthy are suitable for use on their own.

But a more balanced cider can be made by using proportions of bitter-sweets, low in acid content but high in tannin, such as Dabinett and Yarlington Mill, with dessert apples (medium acid and low in tannin) such as Worcester Pearmain, Cox's Orange Pippin, Golden Delicious and so on. Bramley's seedling and other sharp apples are best used for making wine.

Blends are a matter of personal choice. Generally, two parts of medium-sharp apples to one part sweet and one part bitter-sweet apples will give a well-balanced cider. To ensure that the cider is not thin and unattractive, do not use unripe apples. Better to use only good-quality, ripe fruit which has been allowed to lie in a heap for a few days so that the apples start to soften, since this increases the juice yield.

Perry

Perry is to pears what cider is to apples. But because pears are sweeter than apples, sugar need not necessarily be added to the fermentation.

Perry, made from pears, was never as popular as cider, which seems curious in view of the very long life of the pear tree. Some specimens are known to be around 400 years old.

Use perry pears because culinary pears are too mild in flavour.

The recipes for cider can be used for making perries, substituting pears for apples.

> **Pear**
> Wherever the soil is suitable for cider apples, pears, suitable for perry production, will also flourish. In Germany, perry is more popular than cider. There are also big perry orchards in Herefordshire, Gloucestershire and Worcestershire, and in parts of Somerset, Kent and Monmouthshire.

Simple cider

This is a delightfully easy recipe for a pleasing and refreshing drink.

1 kg (2 lb) medium sharp apples
500 g (1 lb) sweet apples
500 g (1 lb) bitter apples
7 litres (1½ gall) water
500 g (1 lb) sugar
2 Campden tablets
2 lemons
yeast

Chop the unpeeled apples into small pieces (including the cores), and put them through a mincer. Put the pulp into a large bowl and cover with 7 litres (1½ gall) water, in which the Campden tablets have been dissolved. Add the juice of the lemons. Stir each day for one week. Strain the liquid into the fermenting vessel and add the yeast. Cover and leave to ferment completely. Afterwards, strain off the cider, leaving the yeast deposit behind. Bottle and leave for four months. If your patience will stand it, leave it longer: the cider will improve.

Cottage cider 1

5 kg (10 lb) windfall apples
500 g (1 lb) raisins
4 litres (7 pints) water
500 g (1 lb) white sugar
3 Campden tablets
yeast

Wash and slice the fruit and raisins into a fermenting vessel containing 4 litres (7 pints) water in which the sugar and Campden tablets have already been dissolved. Leave overnight and add the yeast. Cover with cling wrap and store at a constant temperature of 18-21°C (65-70°F). When fermentation is complete, strain the mixture through muslin into glass storage jars, leaving the yeast deposit behind. Store in filled jars in a cool place for several months until the cider is quite clear. Siphon off again from the yeast deposit and bottle. Leave for a few weeks before drinking.

Cottage cider 2

1 kg (2 lb) windfall apples
750 g (1½ lb) white sugar
2 lemons
2 oranges
2 Campden tablets
water
yeast

Dissolve the Campden tablets and sugar in 3·5 litres (6 pints) water. Grate the apples and add to the water. Extract the juice of the lemons and the oranges and add to the mixture. Add enough water to bring the volume up to 5 litres (1 gall). Chop the orange and lemon peel and add to the vessel. Leave overnight and then add the yeast and cover. Proceed as for cottage cider (1).

Mead

This honey-based drink is one of the most ancient known to man but, rather surprisingly, it has been completely overwhelmed in more recent times by other potions and brews.

Mead originated in Northern Europe, and was a favourite drink of the Norsemen, the Celts, the Irish, the Picts and the Scots. Indeed, we derive our modern word 'honeymoon' from the Norsemen's habit of carousing for a full lunar month after a wedding—drinking, of course, mead.

Despite the recent eclipse of mead, it is pleasant to think that King Arthur and his Knights of the Round Table, if they ever existed, must have celebrated their valiant deeds by drinking mead.

There is every reason to suppose that mead was being drunk 10,000 years ago. The first fermentations may well have been accidental— perhaps some rainwater fell into a store of wild honey and accidentally fermented. Rather than throw the liquid out, some thrifty housewife may have forced her unwilling husband to drink it. The resulting effects would have encouraged subsequent mixings of honey and water. It is possible that mead was discovered in this way.

Honey, the basis of mead, consists of 77 per cent sugar and 17·5 per cent water, together with mineral salts with traces of acids, vitamins, pollen and waxes.

The flowers from which the nectar is extracted affect the flavour of honey. Certain honeys, such as eucalyptus honey, are unsuitable for mead-making.

Play safe and use a light honey.

A word of warning: never allow the must (honey dissolved in hot water) to boil. Honey contains wax and other unwanted ingredients that can adversely affect the quality of the mead. These are partially extracted by dissolving the honey in warm water and very slowly bringing the must to the boil. As soon as boiling point is reached, the pan must be removed from the heat. Skim the unwanted ingredients off the must and allow it to cool.

Dry mead

1·5 kg (3 lb) light honey
3·5 litres (6 pints) water
20 g ($\frac{3}{4}$ oz) citric acid
1 nutrient tablet
1 ml ($\frac{1}{4}$ teaspoon) tannin
maury yeast

Dissolve the honey in the warmed water. The specific gravity should be 1·085. If it is lower than this, add a little more honey. If it is too high, add a little more water. Bring the must to the boil very slowly and skim the unwanted ingredients off the top. Allow the liquid to cool and add the citric acid, the nutrient tablet, tannin and yeast. Transfer to the fermenting vessel and cover. When fermentation is complete, siphon into storage jars and keep in a cool place for six weeks. Bottle and keep for at least six months.

The predominant acid in the lemon is citric and this may constitute five per cent (or even more) of the fresh weight of the juice, which is also particularly rich in Vitamin C and smaller amounts of Vitamin B.

Given the right climate, lemon trees bloom throughout the year and the fruit can be picked up to ten times a year. A really productive lemon tree, under ideal conditions, can produce as many as 7,000 lemons a year.

It was certainly being cultivated in the Azores in 1494. Most of the islands' output was shipped to England. Lemons are now grown throughout the Mediterranean countries.

Party drinks

In this section, we have included a variety of hot and cold drinks which are ideal for any festive occasion. They range from non-alcoholic or slightly alcoholic punches to spicy, pungent mulls for wet, winter evenings. All of them are easy to make and quick to serve.

Do not be afraid to experiment with the recipes. If you have a particularly sweet tooth, add a little honey or sugar; if you prefer a tang, squeeze more lemon juice into the brew. The spiced wines and the syrups may be diluted with hot water, while a bottle of lemonade or ginger ale will dilute a cold drink. You may even like to invent a new punch and join the ranks of the other famous punch-innovators, such as Colonel Negus, who lived in the reign of Queen Anne and devised that well-known drink based on hot spiced port, or Dr Johnson who put claret to such fine use in the drink that now bears his name. Many punches and mulls have an interesting history and have provided for much merry-making and revelry over the centuries. There are no indications at present that this lively trend will cease.

WI Books Ltd. are indebted to the following for providing certain of the party drinks recipes:
Amateur Wine-maker: barbecue cup, pineapple cup, Christmas mull, twelfth night.
Barbara Buchanan, *Bristol Evening Post:* cider cocktail, Bristol hot punch.
Professor George Suchtsbury: claret cup.
Christina Foyle: pink peach, Riesling cup, sherry shiver, snake bite, Christmas punch.
Deinhards: summer bowl.
Cyril Ray: Madeira mull, spiced ale.
Colonel Negus: negus

Non-alcoholic or slightly alcoholic drinks

Fruit cup

equal measures of:
bitter lemon
bitter orange
American dry ginger ale

Mix the ingredients together and serve with pieces of sliced fresh or canned fruit.

Orange punch

500 ml (1 pint) ginger ale
500 ml (1 pint) soda water
225 ml (1 cup) orange juice
100 ml ($\frac{1}{2}$ cup) lemon juice
sugar syrup to taste

Mix the ingredients in a jug and serve in mugs with ice cubes and very thin slices of orange.

Island punch

5 litres (1 gall) ginger ale
2·5 litres ($\frac{1}{2}$ gall) orangeade
225 ml (1 cup) crushed pineapple cubes and juice

Make ice cubes with 1 litre (2 pints) of the ginger ale. Chill the pineapple and remaining ginger ale and orangeade. Mix the ingredients before serving and garnish with thin slices of orange and sprigs of mint.

Pussyfoot

1 small piece of orange
1 small piece of lemon
25 ml (1$\frac{1}{2}$ tablespoons) orange squash
25 ml (1$\frac{1}{2}$ tablespoons) lemon squash
4 drops grenadine syrup
soda water

Put the fruit and grenadine in a tumbler and leave for a few minutes. Measure out the squash and add soda water to taste. Chill and serve.

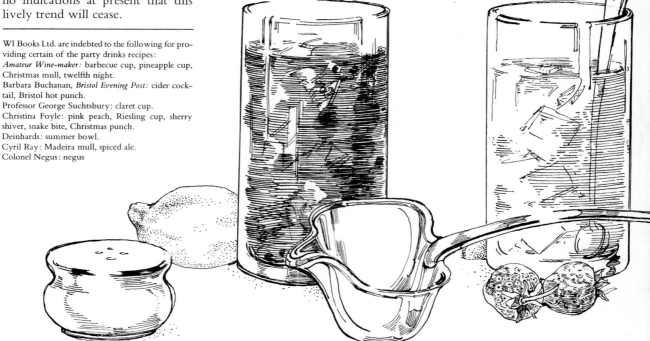

Strawberry delight

strawberries
1 lemon
white sugar
water

Mash the strawberries and pass them through a hair sieve. To every 1·15 litres (2 pints) pulp, add an equal amount of water with sugar to taste. Add the juice and grated rind of the lemon, and stir until the sugar dissolves. Re-strain and serve with lots of ice.

Cider cup 1

1 litre (2 pints) sparkling cider
1 litre (2 pints) soda water
6 oranges
20 ml (2 dessertspoons) sugar

Extract the juice from the oranges. Dissolve the sugar in the juice and add cider and soda water.

> The crusaders helped to spread the cultivation of lemons after they discovered the fruit growing in the Holy Land.

Midsummer's day cooler

250 ml ($\frac{1}{2}$ pint) frozen orange juice
250 ml ($\frac{1}{2}$ pint) ginger ale
125 ml ($\frac{1}{4}$ pint) unsweetened pineapple juice
125 ml ($\frac{1}{4}$ pint) Maraschino juice
1 family sized block vanilla ice cream
15 ml (1 tablespoon) light honey

Mix the orange, pineapple, lemon and Maraschino juices. Add the ginger ale and stir in the honey. Put in the refrigerator and when well-chilled add half the ice cream and blend. Pour into tall glasses. Add 15 ml (1 tablespoon) ice cream to each glass. Garnish with sliced Maraschino cherries if desired.

Lime delight

1 litre (1$\frac{1}{2}$ pints) diluted lime juice
1 can of pears
1 lemon
lemon slices
ice cubes

Strain the juice from the pears and mix with the lime juice and the juice of the lemon. Serve in tall glasses filled with ice and garnish.

Savoury cocktail

500 ml (1 pint) tomato juice
1 lemon
15 ml (1 tablespoon) Worcestershire sauce
45 ml (3 tablespoons) very dry sherry
salt and pepper

Extract the juice from the lemon and mix with the tomato juice, sauce and sherry. Season to taste and serve immediately.

Black beauty

100 ml (6 tablespoons) blackberry juice
100 ml (6 tablespoons) blackcurrant juice
500 ml (1 pint) water
4 lemons
ice

Extract the juice from the lemons and mix with the fruit juices and water. Chill and serve in ice-filled glasses.

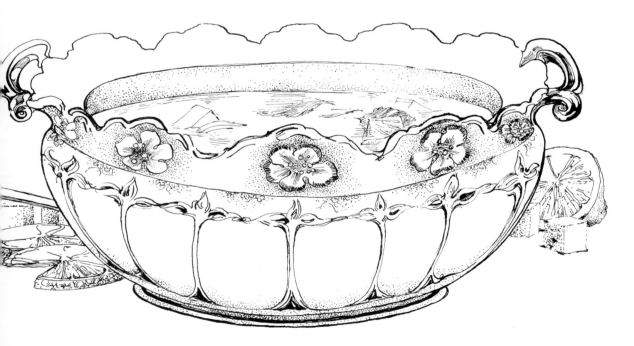

Cider cup 2

1 bottle dry cider (or perry)
1 large tumbler sherry
150 g (5 oz) lump sugar
1 lemon

For a dry cup, omit the sugar and
slice the lemon into the cider and
sherry mixture. Otherwise, peel the
lemon rind (having removed pith),
and leave it in the sherry for an hour.
Dissolve the sugar and lemon juice
in the cider and mix in the sherry.
Serve well chilled.

Cold cup

1 bottle claret
3 large apples
3 large lemons
sugar

Peel, core and slice the apples. Slice
the lemons and put alternate layers
of apple and lemon into a bowl,
covering each layer with a little
sugar. Pour on a bottle of claret and
leave for one hour. Strain into
glasses and serve with ice.

Sangria

1 bottle red wine
1 wineglass brandy (optional)
½ lemon (sliced with peel)
½ orange (sliced with peel)
15 ml (1 tablespoon) white sugar

Mix all the ingredients in a glass jug
and stir. Keep in the refrigerator for
two to three hours before serving.
Serve in tall glasses over lots of ice.

Alcoholic party drinks

These are drinks with a significant alcohol content.

Barbecue cup

5 litres (1 gall) cider
5 litres (1 gall) peach or apricot wine
3 large bottles of white wine
½ bottle brandy

Simply mix all the ingredients together and serve in large goblets, garnished with thinly sliced oranges, mint and ice cubes.

Cider cocktail

5 parts cider
1 part sherry
1 part gin
¼ part lemon squash
a few drops of Angostura bitters

Mix the ingredients, shake well and serve well iced.

Cider cup 1

10 parts sparkling cider
1 part lime juice cordial

Mix and serve well iced and garnished with sprigs of mint.

Cider cup 2

10 parts sparkling cider
1 part orange squash
1 part sweet vermouth

Mix and serve well iced and garnished with slices of orange.

Summer special

1 bottle white wine
125 ml (¼ pint) lemon squash
125 ml (¼ pint) orange squash
1 orange
1 stick of cinnamon
3 cloves
pinch ground nutmeg
soda water

Grate the orange rind and mix with the cloves, cinnamon and nutmeg in the squashes. Simmer for ten minutes. Strain and cool. Add the white wine and soda water to taste. Serve very cold, garnished with fresh mint.

Buck's fizz

(as devised in the famous London club)

orange juice
champagne

Mix together one part fresh orange juice with one part champagne and serve well chilled.

Pineapple cup

125 ml (¼ pint) kirsch
2 bottles dry white wine
50 g (2 oz) sugar
1 small pineapple
1 lemon

Peel the pineapple and discard the peelings. Slice the peeled fruit thinly into a bowl. Add the sugar and kirsch and leave for one hour. Squeeze the lemon and add the juice and some ice. Stir to dissolve the sugar. Mix in the wine and serve in ice-filled glasses garnished with mint and slices of cucumber.

The world eats its way through more than three million tonnes of pineapple every year, proof of the popularity of this splendid fruit which was unknown to Europeans until the early sixteenth century.

Black velvet

Guinness
champagne

Mix equal proportions of Guinness and champagne. Serve in silver tankards. (Ordinary stout and cider can be used. The result is drinkable but does not compare with the real thing.)

Champagne cocktail

champagne
brandy
Angostura bitters
lump sugar

Put a lump of sugar in a champagne glass. Add several drops of bitters and 15 ml (1 tablespoon) brandy. Fill the glass with chilled champagne.

Poor man's champagne cocktail

cheap white sparkling wine
bitters
lump sugar

Put one lump of sugar into each glass. Add the bitters and top with wine. (Sparkling fruit wines or flower wines may be substituted.)

Claret cup

1 bottle non-vintage Bordeaux wine
1 bottle sparkling Moselle
thick slices of pineapple
lots of ice

Put all the ingredients into a large bowl and when thoroughly chilled serve, using a ladle, in small punch glasses.

Cold cup

1 bottle dry sherry (madeira can be used)
3 bottles lemonade
ice

Put the ice in a bowl and pour the sherry over it. Add the lemonade just before serving. For extra sweetness use cream sherry or Malmsey madeira.

Goblin cup

½ bottle strong apple wine
1 wineglass gin
1 wineglass orange squash
chilled soda water

Mix the wine, gin and squash in a jug and top up with soda water as required.

Lafayette punch

1 bottle Moselle
3 bottles champagne
6 oranges
sugar
ice

Slice the oranges into a bowl and sprinkle well with sugar. Add masses of ice and the Moselle. Leave for one hour and add the champagne just before serving.

Orange cardinal

1 bottle champagne
500 ml (1 pint) white wine
100 g (4 oz) sugar
1 orange

Wash and dry the orange. Peel it and scrape off the white pith. Slice the peeled fruit, remove the pips and cover with sugar. Put the rind into the white wine and infuse for eight hours. Strain the wine over the sweetened orange slices and add the champagne just before serving.

Pink peach

1 bottle rosé wine
1 bottle sauternes (or any sweet white wine)
1 miniature peach brandy
125 ml (¼ pint) soda water
1 sliced peach

Pour the rosé wine over a small block of ice and add the fruit. Stir in the sweet wine, peach brandy and sweeten to taste. Chill and add the soda just before serving.

Riesling cup

3 bottles Riesling
2 miniatures Grand Marnier
6 bottles bitter orange
1 packet frozen strawberries

Slice the strawberries into a bowl. Add the wine and the Grand Marnier. Mix well. Add at least ten cubes of ice. Pour in the bitter orange and serve when chilled.

Sherry shiver

1 bottle sherry
1 bottle ginger beer
ice

Mix the sherry and ginger beer. Add the ice and serve when well chilled.

Snake bite

$\frac{1}{3}$ part green ginger wine
$\frac{2}{3}$ part sparkling cider or Babycham

Mix and serve with lots of ice.

Summer bowl

2 bottles light still Riesling
$\frac{1}{2}$ bottle sparkling wine
2 small bottles soda water
1 pineapple
castor sugar

Peel the pineapple and slice. Sprinkle with castor sugar and just cover with enough Riesling. Leave for half an hour well iced and then add the rest of the wine and the soda. Serve well chilled.

Magic flute

(So called because after a few of these you should be hearing music.)

1 bottle gin
1 bottle Dubonnet
3 lemons
soda water

Mix the gin and Dubonnet in a tall jug. Slice the lemons and add to the jug. Top up with soda water and serve well chilled.

Sunset punch

3 bottles well chilled rosé wine
1 bottle gin
60 ml (4 tablespoons) rosehip syrup
1 small bottle Maraschino cherries

Fill a large bowl with ice cubes and add all the ingredients. Mix well and serve immediately.

Mint julep

1 bottle sherry
75 g (3 oz) honey
1 sprig fresh mint
crushed ice

Put the ice and honey in a jug. Sprinkle in the freshly chopped mint. Pour in the wine and serve immediately.

Gin fizz

1 bottle gin
60 ml (4 tablespoons) lemon juice
4 whipped egg whites
sugar
soda water

Blend all the ingredients and add the sugar and soda to taste.

Orange julep

2 bottles sparkling white wine
1 kg (2 pints) sweetened orange juice
10 ml (1 dessertspoon) Angostura bitters
2 large oranges
fresh mint sprigs

Wash and thinly slice the oranges. Put them in a bowl and pour in the orange juice. Stir in the bitters, ice and wine. Pour the chilled mixture into tall glasses garnished with fresh mint.

Hot punches

Do not overheat punch as the alcohol will evaporate.

Simple punch

2 bottles red wine
2 bottles white wine
¼ bottle rum
1 orange
2 apples
cloves

Spike the orange with the cloves and roast with the peelings of the two apples. Heat the wine in a saucepan and float in the roasted orange when the liquid begins to steam. Just before serving, remove from the heat and stir in the rum.

Bristol hot punch

1 bottle burgundy
1 bottle cider
1 bottle water
1 can grapefruit juice
30 ml (2 tablespoons) brown sugar
2 apples
2 satsuma oranges
grapes
nutmeg

Heat all the liquids to near boiling point. While this is happening, slice the apples and the oranges. Skin the grapes. When the liquid is near boiling, turn down the heat and simmer with the fruit. Sprinkle with nutmeg just before serving.

Christmas punch

1 large bottle Dubonnet
1 bottle red wine
500 ml (1 pint) freshly infused China tea
juice of ½ lemon
juice of ½ orange
5 ml (1 teaspoon) cinnamon
nutmeg
3 cloves
twist of lemon peel
brown sugar

Boil the fruit juice, thinly peeled rinds, cinnamon, nutmeg, cloves and sugar in a saucepan with the strained tea. Simmer for 15 minutes and strain into a second pan. Add the Dubonnet and red wine. Heat quickly (without boiling) and serve in a warmed punch-bowl, decorated with thinly sliced oranges and lemons.

Orange

Oranges owed their early popularity and wide cultivation to the conquest of the Roman Empire, the Arab trade routes, the expansion of Islam around the Mediterranean and to the crusades of the Middle Ages.

Oranges are believed to be native to the tropical regions of Asia and particularly to the Malaysian archipelago.

Columbus introduced oranges into the western hemisphere when he established a settlement in Hispaniola in 1493. They were by that time common in the Canary Islands. The first reference to orange seeds being planted in America occurs in an old manuscript written in 1518.

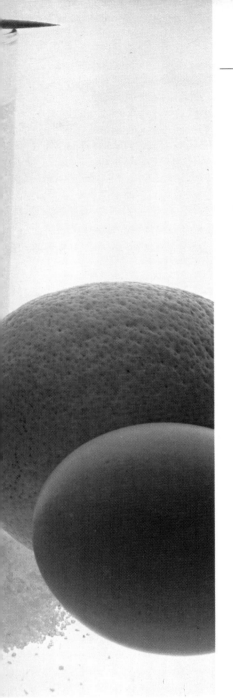

Cider cooler

1 bottle cider
450 ml (16 fl oz) dry sherry
1 lemon
ice

Mix the cider and the sherry. Fill a suitably sized jug with crushed ice and pour the cider and sherry over the ice. Add the juice of the lemons and stir well.

Christmas mull

1 bottle elderberry wine
225 g (4 oz) granulated sugar
225 g (8 fl oz) water
2 lemons
4 cloves
4 sticks cinnamon

Boil the mixture of sugar, spices and water for five minutes, add the thinly sliced lemon and allow to stand for ten minutes. Add the wine, heat slowly just short of boiling and serve hot.

Cider punch

5 litres (1 gall) draught cider
½ bottle rum
2 oranges
1 lemon
1 piece of root ginger
1 sprig rosemary
cloves

Halve the oranges and spike with cloves. Grate the lemon peel. Add the cider to the lemon peel and orange and simmer with the crushed ginger and rosemary. When the liquid is simmering, add the rum and sweeten to taste.

Dr Johnson's punch

1 litre (2 pints) claret
1 wineglass curaçao
1 wineglass brandy
500 ml (1 pint) water
2 oranges
6 cloves
1 ml (¼ teaspoon) grated nutmeg
lump sugar

Heat the claret with the sliced oranges, 12 lumps of sugar and the cloves. When the liquid is near to boiling, add 500 ml (1 pint) boiling water, the curaçao and the brandy. Grate the nutmeg on top and serve steaming hot.

Specifick

1 bottle dry white wine
2 wineglasses brandy
juice of 1 lemon
60 ml (6 dessertspoons) light honey

Put all the ingredients in a saucepan, mix while heating to near-boiling and serve hot.

Julglogg

This Swedish recipe requires aquavit, but gin can be used if aquavit is not readily available.

1 bottle aquavit
2 bottles burgundy
75 g (3 oz) raisins
75 g (3 oz) white sugar
15 ml (1 tablespoon) cardamom seeds
5 cloves
3 sticks cinnamon
1 small piece lemon peel
blanched almonds

Put the spices and lemon peel in a cheesecloth and place in a saucepan with half the aquavit, all the burgundy, the raisins and the sugar. Cover the pan and simmer for 30 minutes. Add the remaining aquavit. For a spectacular effect, dim the lights and ignite the julglogg. Serve the flaming liquid, using a long-handled spoon, in punch glasses containing a few blanched almonds.

Madeira mull

1 bottle madeira
30 ml (2 tablespoons) brandy
pinch cinnamon
pinch ginger
sugar

Heat all the ingredients in a saucepan to just below boiling point. Simmer for a few minutes before serving.

stable	a wine in which all the sugar has fermented is said to be stable; certain chemicals can stabilize a wine by preventing further fermentation	**tannin**	a naturally occurring substance found in the skins and stems of fruit; the higher the tannin content of the base fruit, the more astringent or bitter the wine
sulphur dioxide	a sterilizing agent that kills spoilage yeast and bacteria; it is the principal component of Campden tablets		
sulphiting	adding sulphur dioxide to wine, and so causing it to stabilize; Campden tablets are used to achieve this	**vinegar fly**	a fruit fly that causes wine to turn into vinegar; it is prevented from entering the fermentation jar by a fermentation trap
stuck	a wine has stuck when it has stopped fermenting too early; usually it is caused by an inactive yeast; to prevent a stuck fermentation, ensure that your yeast is young and fresh	**yeast nutrient**	ammonium sulphate, a chemical used to stimulate the yeast in fermentation

Conversion Tables

All weights and measures in this book are given in the metric system, followed by the imperial in brackets. Conversions are correctly adjusted within one system and have been taken up or down to round figures in all instances to make for ease of working. Do not worry if you find the conversions differ slightly from those given in the tables here, which are for general reference only. Providing you follow one set of measures—*either* the imperial *or* the metric—these variations are of no importance. Do not attempt to mix the measurements in any recipe, or the amounts will not be correctly adjusted.

Weights

Metric	Imperial
7 g	$\frac{1}{4}$ oz
12 g	$\frac{1}{2}$ oz
25 g	1 oz
100-125 g	4 oz
225 g	8 oz
450 g	1 lb
900 g	2 lb
1 kg	2 lb 3 oz

Liquid Measures

Metric	Imperial
25 ml	1 fl oz
50 ml	2 fl oz
75 ml	3 fl oz
100 ml	4 fl oz
275 ml	$\frac{1}{2}$ pint
575 ml	1 pint
1 litre	$1\frac{3}{4}$ pints
4.5 litres	1 gallon

Index

Recipes